"Time to discard the small do's and don'ts notes you've been carrying around for years...finally a book that captures the art of how to 'sell' with the art of how to 'tell' in a succinct and straightforward guide; complete with key tips that provide all you need to know about giving oral presentations to effectively communicate the value of your organization to a potential client. Having led captures and organizations from \$5 M to \$5B over 34 years, this is a must-read for capture leaders, capture teams, and business leaders alike."

John Mengucci
CACI Chief Operating Officer
Former Lockheed Martin Business Executive

"John Parker Stewart has an uncanny ability to instill confidence, bring out genuineness, and ensure clarity and conciseness of delivery, that when combined together will help any individual or team deliver a compliant, compelling, and ultimately winning oral proposal presentation."

Mark Gray
President and CEO, ASRC Federal

"*Mastering the Art of Oral Presentations* fills an absolutely critical need in the area of winning new business. In coauthoring this book, Don Fulop has synthesized over 40 years of highly successful engineering, program management, and business development expertise. He was consistently the 'winningest' business development executive I knew at Lockheed Martin. His knowledge of the secret ins and outs of structuring oral presentations, meticulous preparation, and rehearsal for key customer orals, and highly skilled performance in front of senior acquisition executives were major contributing factors in his many multibillion-dollar program wins. Don set the industry standard for orals and customer presentations, and in *Mastering the Art of Oral Presentations* he shares his secrets with the reader. This book is essential to any library on how to win business."

Benjamin H. Schleider III, PhD
CEO, DCG LLC
Former Lockheed Martin Executive

"Great ideas are often challenging to communicate. *Mastering the Art of Oral Presentations* provides easy-to-grasp tools to ensure a smart, persuasive, and dynamic presentation."

Devon Burt
VP/Creative Director, Apparel Special Projects, Nike

"Presenting a cogent oral argument—be it to an auditorium full of strangers, a classroom of distracted teenagers, a gathering of superiors and peers, a courtroom with a judge and jury, a job interview, or a selection board of potential clients—is equal parts art, science, and, at its best, pure, unforgettable magic. The stakes are usually high and you get only a single shot at persuading the target audience. How to make the most of that one opportunity is what this book is all about. Don Fulop and John Parker Stewart truly stand up and deliver. They lift the veil and reveal what magicians rarely, if ever, share: their real secrets. Anchored in decades of highly successful experience at the pinnacle of business development—itself a mercurial combo of art, science, and magic—at such top-tier companies as Lockheed Martin and CACI, Don Fulop's perspective offers the invaluable insight, realism, and grit of the skilled practitioner. He has been there and done that—skillfully, gracefully, and seemingly effortlessly—delivering uncommon results. He has led, educated, inspired, pushed, cajoled, delighted, and amazed even in the face of doubts, vacillations, and the inevitable resistance to change. He is an experienced guide who knows both the path to success and the obstacles along the way. With Don at the helm, the sky is no limit. John Parker Stewart, the indomitable executive coach and supreme motivator, always brings out the best in individuals and teams. Together, Fulop and Stewart are an unbeatable combination. They deliver a readable, relevant and compelling book. *Mastering the Art of Oral Presentations* isn't 'Public Speaking for Dummies' or yet another generic 'how to' book. Listen to their voices of experience, learn their keys to success, and you too might be able to make magic happen."

Dr. Lani Kass
Senior Vice President and Corporate Strategic Advisor, CACI International Inc.
Former Senior Policy Advisor to the Chairman of the Joint Chiefs of Staff
Former Special Assistant to the Chief, USAF
Former Professor of Military Strategy at the National War College

"The business leader must never forget that a customer's request for orals is an open invitation to differentiate their offering from all others. Stewart's experience and practical tools, when combined with hard work and preparation, provide everything you need for successful orals with high impact and solid substance."

Dan Olson
VP/GM, Northrop Grumman, Armament Systems Division

"Don Fulop is uniquely qualified to coauthor this book. His skill as an accomplished engineer, coupled with a special talent for visualizing the winning elements of a difficult proposal and understanding of the added value of a properly developed oral presentation, have resulted in a highly respected reputation in the technical business development community."

Jay Honeycutt
Former Director, NASA Kennedy Space Center
President, Lockheed Martin Space Operations

"It is fantastic that John has shared his vast knowledge and experience in oral presentations through this comprehensive and compelling book enabling the reader to win more often."

Ray Kiley, CEO, Intelledox

"Facing an oral presentation is much feared and all too often deferred, but is an increasingly critical aspect of winning proposals. How to succeed is put squarely under the microscope by John Parker Stewart and Don Fulop. Rest assured the winning organization will have thoroughly studied this invaluable resource."

Colonel James C. Adamson, US Army, Ret.
NASA Astronaut
Former President, Lockheed Martin
Former CEO, Allied Signal/Honeywell

"This book is packed with world-class tips on speaking and presenting by a world-class coach. John is the *best!*"

Tarek Robbiati
Former CFO, Sprint
Former CEO, CSL-Hong Kong

"If you are a professional who has to win a proposal or impress a prospective client, this book should be a must-read for you and your team. I had the opportunity to work with Don Fulop in the highly competitive federal services contracting world and he is one of the real winners in this space. His focus on the strategy for what it takes to win, his clarity of offer, and mostly to the preparation for the presentations that are increasingly a part of large, must-win, proposals, Don is a proven leader. As we competed to grow from our base of a successful $2.5 billion company, leaving a presentation to chance was not an option. Don's proven techniques, and ability to teach these to a broad group of colleagues, really sets him apart and made his "Will to Win" a key differentiator. I would strongly endorse this as a must-read for anyone who wants to increase their probability of win."

Mike Thomas
Former President, Lockheed Martin IS&GS Security Group

"John is on the extremely short list of orals coaches who have an uncanny ability to instantaneously connect with key leaders and orals teams in a credible way. He enables them to communicate effectively, serving not only their own best interests, but the best interests of the organizations that they seek to serve in a superior way."

Brian Dalton
Vice President, Human Resources, KBRwyle
Former CHRO, Orbital ATK

"John's ability to find and articulate the essentials of a successful orals team is masterfully explained in a way that is understandable and executable by all levels. This is a must-read for anyone involved in oral presentations."

David J. Dacquino
Chairman and CEO, Serco Inc.
Former Senior VP & GM, Raytheon Technical Services Co.

"Oral presentation success is a vital part of the implementation of marketing strategies. This in turn leads to sales and market growth. This compilation of methods, communication strategies, and presentation planning can be used by nearly any company or organization to produce excellent oral presenters. John's insight and leadership methods have proven over the years to be consistently successful. I have used many of these methods to improve sales, marketing, and customer interface for over 20 years. I fully endorse this book and the methods described therein to produce excellent oral presenters, the backbone of sales and market share growth."

Brian K. Hovik
Market Manager, Aerospace – BASF Corporation
Former Senior Engineer – Boeing Research & Development

"How to prepare, practice, and present for an oral's presentation … this book is written by the experts and has the secrets for your team's success."

Carey Smith
President, Parsons Corporation Federal Business Unit

"When your business growth depends on the ability to articulate why potential clients should choose your company over the competition, John Parker Stewart's oral coaching methods and strategies provide the definitive approach to success. This invaluable tool is also 100% applicable to businesses outside the government sector, and to anyone wanting to hone their presentation and analytical skills."

Richard B. Evans
President and CEO, Health Care Solutions International

"Persuasion is the name of the game! John Parker Stewart and Don Fulop have crafted a masterful book to successfully take the reader to that goal."

Dr. Cynthia Z.F. Clark
Former Administrator, National Agricultural Statistics Service, USDA

"John Parker Stewart's unique ability to combine both the business and human aspects into a presentation is second to none. This book provides the needed guidance for all competing oral teams to deliver persuasive and credible presentations. It is a must to capture targeted contracts."

Daniel Cox
CEO, GCR Inc., New Orleans

"I fully endorse *Mastering the Art of Oral Presentations*! John Parker Stewart and Don Fulop have captured all the essentials of a successful orals that will help any competing team win their targeted contract!"

David Clark
COO, SC3

"Nobody in the world better understands the art and science of delivering a government oral presentation than John Parker Stewart and Don Fulop. They have worked with thousands of presenters over the decades, resulting in countless wins. They truly understand how to make you victorious! *Mastering the Art of Oral Presentations* provides you with the essential ingredients to make a winning presentation. Fulop and Stewart have crafted a masterpiece. This book is a staple for any executive who plans on doing business with the government, as well as all professionals who need to polish their presentation skills."

Holton Yost
General Manager, General Dynamics Information Technology

Mastering the Art of Oral Presentations is undoubtedly the most comprehensive book available to prepare effective presentations that deliver results in any business situation … with its time-tested and practical coaching advice spread throughout, you will find it indispensable."

Michael Millane
Principal Program Manager, Intel Corporation

"To master an orals presentation and gain a competitive advantage, this is a kick-ass, must-read book! Stewart and Fulop have written the essential primer for anyone venturing into the perilous world of orals presentations. To overcome your insecurity and desperation in making that big presentation, read this book again and again, and learn from the best!"

J. Willian Koegel, Jr.
Executive Vice President, General Counsel & Secretary, CACI
Former Partner, Steptoe & Johnson
Former Member, DC Legal Ethics Committee—Washington, DC

"John Parker Stewart successfully blends the art and science of oral presentations, and shares a piece of his magic in *Mastering the Art of Oral Presentations*. I have worked with John, and experienced his magic first-hand. Having worked with many orals coaches, there is no other coach in his league, and no process that comes close! I highly recommend his approach to individuals and teams facing any type of orals. His process and tools create confident teams and compelling presentations!"

Sue Shaffer
VP-Business Development, SGT

"Composing an interesting story and telling it in a compelling way are the keys to *any* successful presentation. John Parker Stewart and Don Fulop offer their performance-proven methods to guide you in delivering your next winning presentation."

Rear Admiral Mark A. Hugel, US Navy (ret.)

MASTERING THE ART OF

ORAL PRESENTATIONS

JOHN PARKER STEWART
DON FULOP

MASTERING THE ART OF
ORAL
PRESENTATIONS

WINNING ORALS, SPEECHES, AND STAND-UP PRESENTATIONS

WILEY

For general information on our other products and services or for technical support, please contact our Customer Care Department within the United States at (800) 762-2974, outside the United States at (317) 572-3993 or fax (317) 572-4002.

Wiley publishes in a variety of print and electronic formats and by print-on-demand. Some material included with standard print versions of this book may not be included in e-books or in print-on-demand. If this book refers to media such as a CD or DVD that is not included in the version you purchased, you may download this material at http://booksupport.wiley.com. For more information about Wiley products, visit www.wiley.com.

Library of Congress Cataloging-in-Publication Data

Names: Stewart, John Parker, author. | Fulop, Don, 1950- author.
Title: Mastering the art of oral presentations : winning orals, speeches, and
    stand-up presentations / John Parker Stewart, Don Fulop.
Description: Hoboken, New Jersey : Wiley, [2019] | Includes index. |
    Identifiers: LCCN 2018050992 (print) | LCCN 2018056145 (ebook) | ISBN
    9781119550129 (ePub) | ISBN 9781119550105 (ePDF) | ISBN 9781119550051 |
    ISBN 9781119550051(hardcover) | ISBN 9781119550105(ePDF) | ISBN
    9781119550129(ePub)
Subjects: LCSH: Public speaking. | Oral communication. | Business
    communication.
Classification: LCC PN4129.15 (ebook) | LCC PN4129.15 .S74 2019 (print) | DDC
    808.5/1–dc23
LC record available at https://lccn.loc.gov/2018050992

Printed in the United States of America
V10008305_022019

Contents

Foreword

In the pursuit of large government contracts, it is common that each competitor be required to make a face-to-face or video presentation to a source selection board. These oral presentations usually require that the key personnel of each competitor's team explain how they will meet or exceed the customer's expectations as the winning contractor.

Oral presentations are one of the most nerve-wracking experiences any professional must endure! Every word spoken carries the same weight as a written proposal. In addition to leveraging technical content, your presenters must impress and convince the source selection board that your team is the one that will best meet all of their requirements and the one they want to work with for years to come.

Having worked in the government contracting industry for over 40 years, I have learned that oral presentations require a completely different set of skills from the ones needed for producing a written proposal. Knowing that "you never get a second chance at a first impression," it is imperative to seek the best advice and coaching to make the most of the opportunity for presenting your ideas to your prospective customers.

Two of my favorite people, John Parker Stewart and Don Fulop, have now collaborated on *Mastering the Art of Oral Presentations*, a clear and comprehensive guide that covers every facet of preparing your oral presentation team to make the absolute most of their time in front of the customer.

John Parker Stewart, an internationally renowned author and executive skills development coach, adapted all his learning about what works and what doesn't for highly effective communication to provide key steps for preparing and delivering remarkable oral presentations.

John joined forces with Don Fulop, who is one of the finest, most successful business development executives who has ever pursued and won federal government contracts. The fruit of their collaboration is a complete game plan for preparing, practicing with, and delivering successful oral presentations for federal government contracts. In fact, the principals and practices detailed in this book are equally applicable to any oral presentation, speech, or stand-up presentation.

Within the covers of this invaluable guide, you will find all the support, tips, and advice you will need for developing an oral presentation from start to finish. The process that Don and John outline will help you understand, implement, and satisfy the orals requirements for your team and for yourself.

Consider this book an orals coach in one comprehensive volume. Use this guide to learn each phase of the orals requirements. You will find a thorough explanation accompanied by examples of what an orals experience entails, and how to apply it to your specific needs in meeting the requirements you face.

Good luck learning all the ins and outs of an orals experience. You will not receive a more complete and practical guide anywhere than this book will give you! Follow these orals tips from two masters of the trade, and you will be several steps ahead of your competition.

Good luck in winning your next contract! I wish you all the best!

Ken Asbury
CEO and President, CACI

Introduction

An Absolute Will to Win Is Essential for Success

F ormal oral presentations communicate a message in a way that is unlike any other method of delivery. Nothing is more influential than a dynamic, face-to-face presentation followed by a lively discussion among the various stakeholders.

A powerful presentation will endure in the minds of the audience and ultimately become a motivating force that positively influences their decision making. To make your presentation memorable, you must understand what makes people receptive to what you have to say, deliver a credible and convincing message, and stay focused on your topic.

This involves a great deal of deliberate, thorough preparation. It must not be treated as an impromptu event. To ensure the success of your targeted outcome, your presentation must be thoughtfully planned, it must be insightful, and it must be compelling.

This book describes the essential elements, processes, and behaviors needed for preparing and delivering an impactful, enduring formal oral presentation. Its focus is on selling products and services of all types, in both commercial and government buying/procurement applications.

It provides you with sound guidance based on decades of successful, real-world experience and lessons learned. Templates are provided to help you sharpen your presentation. All material covered is applicable to both individual and team presentations. And, when considering winning approaches and strategies, it applies to your professional life and your personal life as well!

Expert tips and instructions are included to help you learn how to win the hearts and minds of your audience. The book describes in detail how to develop and deliver your message to win potential customers, influence people, and ultimately obtain an enthusiastic and reassuring nod from decision makers.

In a selling environment, oral presentations are fundamentally very different from written proposals. Winning oral presentations require much more than merely demonstrating compliance with the customer's requirements or entertaining the audience.

From the perspective of your customer or the people you're attempting to influence, formal oral presentations exist only to help them decide how to best satisfy their goals and objectives. This is a critical part of their decision-making process.

Through interaction with you, your key personnel, and your team, an oral presentation offers a singular opportunity for you to convince the customer that you are uniquely qualified to satisfy their needs. To rise above the competition, your presentation must demonstrate distinctive value that addresses all their requirements, it must be brilliantly easy to understand, and it must be memorable.

There are many common misconceptions about oral presentations. If any one of them influences your presentation planning and preparation process, it can contribute to a less than successful outcome. Potentially toxic assumptions include the following:

- Orals are simply a briefing.
- Orals are a verbal summary of a written proposal or document.

- An orals coach or speech coach isn't required.
- Orals only minimally affect decisions or influence the customer/audience.

Don't allow any of these misconceptions to negatively impact your presentation. Orals are truly unique and present you with an opportunity to shine. Don't fail to capitalize on this opportunity! Understand the principles and processes that winners use to deliver an oral presentation as a powerful differentiator in the eyes of the customer.

Formal oral presentations are not unique to a particular market segment or industry. Just think about how important an oral presentation can be for any purpose. Think about how it ultimately impacts the selection process in the mind of any decision maker.

Most people use a variety of inputs to make decisions, but nothing can influence and connect you with your audience like a successful face-to-face meeting followed by an honest and open discussion. Important facts that could easily be missed via the written word are emphasized, graphics and illustrations are thoroughly described and discussed, questions are answered on the spot, and most importantly, the decision maker experiences first-hand what it's like to work with you.

As you prepare yourself and your team for an oral presentation, remember one thing: an absolute will to win is essential for success. This commitment will energize your proposals and presentations, and it must dominate and drive everything that you do.

Government Orals—What They Are, How They Originated, Why They Are So Important, and the Requirements the Government Must Follow When They Are Used

Understanding Why Orals Became a Part of the Government Procurement Process and How They Are Used Is a Key to Success

The orals process originated in the 1990s when the government determined that orals offered an efficient way to streamline the

procurement process, minimize and clarify outstanding issues associated with the procurement, and improve the overall quality and end
products of the acquisitions. The orals process also allows the government to evaluate the competence of key personnel, understand how
key personnel (including teammates, subcontractors, and vendors)
work together, and although not a formalized requirement, assess
how well the government team feels it can work with the contractor's team. For these reasons, and others discussed in this book, orals
are an exceptionally important part of procurement when they are
called for by the government.

Federal Acquisition Regulation (FAR) 15.102 states that oral
presentations may substitute for or augment, written information
provided by the bidder. Taken to the extreme, this means that the
government may not require a written technical proposal and can
base their entire selection on an oral proposal supplemented by
certifications, representations, and a signed offer sheet (cost/pricing).
Winning the contract can depend entirely upon the responsiveness
and quality of your presentation.

Think of an oral proposal in the same way you would a written
proposal. The contracting officer must establish the ground rules for
the presentation in writing, may record the presentation, and will
score the orally presented information according to the criteria stated
in the solicitation document.

On this point, FAR 15.102(d) states: "When oral presentations
are required, the solicitation shall provide offerors with sufficient
information to prepare them." Accordingly, the government solicitation may describe the following items:

1. The types of information to be presented orally and the associated
   evaluation factors that will be used for scoring.
2. The qualifications for personnel that will be required to provide the
   oral presentation.
3. The requirements for, and any limitations and/or prohibitions on,
   the use of written material or other media to supplement the oral
   presentation.

4. The location, date, and time for the oral presentation.
5. The restrictions governing the time permitted for each oral presentation.
6. The scope and content of exchanges that may occur between the Government's participants and the offeror's representatives as part of the oral presentations, including whether or not discussions (see 15.306(d)) will be permitted during oral presentations.

The Appendix of this book includes the FAR language associated with oral presentations (FAR 15.102). Although there have been few changes to the criteria for orals over the years, it's always a good idea to check the latest release of the FAR to review and understand all current requirements.

Customer's Objectives

Understand the Customer's Direct/Indirect Goals and Objectives

Customers use oral presentations to evaluate any number of formal and informal buying criteria and assist them in their decision-making process. Their goals and expectations include, but may not be limited to, the following:

- Understand proposal content and individual/team competency.
- Assess face-to-face interaction and compatibility with the presentation/implementation team.
- Observe how key personnel
  - Present themselves.
  - Work together.
  - Interact with the customer.
  - Communicate information.
  - Address and answer questions.
- Interview the account manager, program or project manager, and key personnel.
- Test the ability of the team's leadership in a variety of ways.
- Reduce their supplier selection time and cost.

To win, you must be well prepared to address these criteria as carefully and diligently as you would in a written proposal. Complexity arises from the fact that orals are a stage show that must be believable, persuasive, memorable, and engaging. The presenters are the performers, and the audience and evaluators are the customers—the people who will ultimately make or greatly influence the final buying decision.

Designing compelling team presentations that meet your customer's complex needs is much more challenging than preparing and delivering individual presentations. Generally, team presentations require many people, more material is presented, there are more opportunities for errors and inconsistencies across the presentation, and timing can become an issue. For this reason, we will concentrate on team presentations even though every principle and technique described in this book is equally applicable to individual presenters.

Your Team and Your Team's Objectives

Carefully Select Your Team Members Based on Individual Qualifications, Not on Pure Sales or Speaking Skills Alone

An effective presentation team will use orals as an opportunity to:

- Address all your customer's requirements.
- Show that your team understands your customer's needs and desires.
- Demonstrate knowledge, competency, and capabilities.
- Articulate win themes and discriminators.
- Stress strengths.
- Mitigate weaknesses.
- Counter or exceed the competition's strengths.
- Subtly call attention to your competition's weaknesses; also known as "ghosting."
- Demonstrate that your team's leadership, product, or service is the best for your customer.
- Connect with your customer.

Select presenters based on their qualifications, not on their presentation skills. Carefully examine the qualifications that your customer is looking for: the skills needed to perform the work following a contract award combined with demonstrated successful past performance in like environments or situations. There is no substitute for experience when measured against other key qualifications. An orals or speech coach can help you develop winning presentation techniques in days, but there is no way to credibly insert years of valuable experience into an empty resume.

Master's Tip: Build a Winning Team

Team composition, experience, and qualifications are of paramount importance. You must ensure that all key customer-specified qualifications are met and that the people you select have the experience needed to perform on-contract. Without an optimized team, your probability of a win will be greatly diminished.

As the leader of an orals presentation, it's your responsibility to ensure that you have a winning team. If you don't have the right people or if you have people who do not align themselves completely with the overall win strategy, replace them immediately. Don't wait! Don't fool yourself into thinking you can convince the disruptor to "see it your way." The sooner you have a cohesive team with a winning attitude, the better. Your team must work closely together from day one and they must embrace and believe in every aspect of the win strategy. If you sense that a problem exists or is developing, address it immediately.

As you assemble your team, remember that your customer, audience, and evaluators will be looking at, and listening for, key attributes of your team and its approach. Specific questions exist in the customer's mind, and it's your job to ensure they are answered and fully satisfied. Here are just a few of those questions:

- Do the individuals making the presentation work well together as a well-rounded team?
- Is the prime contractor really in charge here? Do their subcontractors and vendors integrate well into this team? Do they complement each other or do they conflict with each other?
- Does the entire team have a clear understanding of what I'm looking for as their customer?
- Can I work well with this team?
- Will this team work with me as issues arise in the future?
- Is this team committed to our mutual success?

Orals Coach or Speech Coach?

When Learning a New Skill or Enhancing an Existing Skill, Use a Professional

A professional orals or speech coach can help to prepare each presenter to deal with the unfamiliar psychological environment that contributes to orals complexity and the angst that most people feel when required to stand up and formally address an audience. A major source of anxiety in every speaker facing a new presentation environment is a fear of "the unknown." Indeed, there are many unknowns to worry about! An experienced orals coach can help to eliminate this fear and put speakers at ease.

There is an important distinction between an orals coach and a speech coach. A speech coach will hone your presentation skills but will not necessarily work the presentation content or your ability to address your customer's needs. An orals coach will not only provide advice and guidance on presentation skills but will also help to ensure your presentation content addresses your customer's needs and specific requirements.

An orals coach will also assist you in understanding how to deal with post-presentation question-and-answer sessions (Q&As). How you respond during a Q&A can easily determine if you will win or lose, regardless of the quality and overall effectiveness of your formal oral presentation or written proposal. Never underestimate the importance of the Q&A, and always ensure that your team is well prepared to deal with it.

In short, an orals coach not only polishes every aspect of your presentation but also addresses compliance with all the customer's needs, including how to respond during the Q&A. In an environment in which the customer is using orals to help reach a decision, these two elements of the presentation—compliance and Q&A responsiveness—are crucial and can make the difference between winning and losing.

The orals coach will guide each presenter to project the following:

- Confidence—the single most important thing that each member of the team must have.
- Expertise in their respective areas.
- Detailed and specific knowledge of the customer's needs and requirements.
- Passion for both the subject and their desire to serve the customer.
- Commitment to the customer's mission.
- Energy, honesty, and sincerity.
- Reliability, responsibility, dependability, and motivation.
- Compatibility with their team and with the customer.
- Soft skills that are designed to engage to the customer include the following:
  - Being convincing, enthusiastic, thorough, and positive.
  - Aligning your thinking and delivery to support and reinforce the messages being articulated.
  - Addressing your appearance, gestures, posture, and ability to clearly project the message.
  - Bringing out your most likable personality traits (and candidly squelching the ones that are detractors).

An effective orals coach will guide you through the proven process described in this book to ensure you address all customer needs and team objectives thoroughly, competently, and in a compelling way that your customer will remember. Your coach will ensure that you are exceptionally well prepared to function professionally, capably, and impressively in a formal orals environment.

Chapter 1

Preparation

Preparation Is the Foundation of Success

Before beginning any work on presentation materials, it is imperative that the presenters share a common understanding of the customer's needs, the team's offering, the competition, and how each of these elements should be addressed to achieve the highest probability of a win. This step is of paramount importance, yet many companies—losing companies—commonly overlook it!

If a written proposal is required prior to making an oral presentation, it's easy to say, "We've submitted a 'winning' written proposal, let's just summarize it and talk about our key points." When required, the written proposal forms a foundation for the oral presentation and is nothing more than that. In general, written proposals are technical and sterile. They are written and prepared using proven processes and strictly follow instructions provided or described by your customer.

Even though you may have submitted an excellent written proposal, winning oral presentations mandate implementation of a creative process that capitalizes on, and launches from, the good work that has been done to date.

As you and your team prepare your oral presentation materials, don't forget that the process of learning more about the competition and the customer never stops until the contract is awarded. You and your team must continue to learn as much as you can as long as you can and leverage these expanding insights to optimize your value proposition for your oral presentation.

Know your customer. Know your competition. Never stop learning as much as you can about either of them.

Customer Intelligence

Thoroughly Understand Your Customer

Demonstrate that you thoroughly understand your customer's needs, their criteria for success, their concerns, and their vision for the future. Your ability to share their interests, alleviate their concerns, and demonstrate that you understand their environment will greatly improve your chance of winning. The customers who are on the source selection committee are decision makers who will select—or recommend to the ultimate decision maker—who wins. Their decision determines your future. Your job is to help them make their decision in your favor.

To win you must know and thoroughly understand your customer and your customer's needs. This means that customer contact must begin early, long before the formal buying process begins. Unless you're selling a generic off-the-shelf product or service, simply responding to a customer's request for quotation or proposal without adequate preparation is, simply put, a loser.

Starting early provides many advantages. Here are just a few:

- Enables you to know and freely interact with your customer before the "formal" buying or acquisition process is initiated. This provides valuable insight on the real issues surrounding the procurement.
- Gives you an opportunity to "help mold" the procurement requirements by pointing out the benefits and disadvantages of different approaches, both strategic and technical, that the customer may not be aware of.
- Provides an opportunity to discuss performance versus cost and schedule constraints.
- Helps the customer know what it's like to work with you.
- May give you insight into the competition.

Master's Tip: Know Who the *Real* Decision Makers Are

You must know who your real customer is. Frequently, sellers erroneously assume that the customers' buyers, purchasing agents, or acquisition people are the decision makers, but they may not be! Find out who the real decision makers are and what their hot buttons are for the procurement. "Hot buttons" refers to items that are a high priority in the customer's mind and will have the greatest impact on their decision-making. Hot buttons may be associated with any number of technical, managerial, cost, or schedule issues. It is your job to find out what the customer's hot buttons are and use this understanding to design your offering. Unless you do this, your chances of preparing a winning presentation and accompanying written proposal will be greatly diminished. Start early, find out who the real customers and decision makers are, find out what their hot buttons are, and never stop communicating with the decision makers until you are requested or required to do so.

Items to consider when gathering and documenting customer intelligence include:

- The buying organization's history, and the history of the current work/program.
- The customer's organization, who the key evaluators are, and who the ultimate decision makers are.
- The incumbent contractor's performance, if applicable.
- The customer's vision, goals, and objectives for this procurement.
- The customer's feelings about your company, your key personnel, and your company's past applicable performance.
- The "external" and "internal" customers, and their requirements.
- The customer's formal and informal priorities.
- Underlying objectives the customer hopes to accomplish.
- Motivation for issuing the Request for Proposal (RFP), Request for Quotation (RFQ), or Purchase Order (PO).
- Political pressures, both internal and external.
- Recent developments that may influence the environment or the solicitation.

- Customer organizational changes, particularly in key positions.
- Technology drivers.
- Short-term, mid-term, and long-term goals.
- Frustrations with previous or current suppliers/contractors, such as the following:
  - Failure to meet contract requirements in terms of technical, cost, or schedule performance.
  - Contractor failure to proactively manage and communicate.
  - Team members, subcontractors, or vendors not performing satisfactorily.
  - Contractors' priorities shifting away from those of the customer.
  - Failure to produce and provide proper and accurate documentation.
  - Lack of depth in the contractor's team.
  - Being caught unaware or surprised by programmatic developments.

In addition to understanding your customer, learn everything you can about their major issues and concerns, for example, worries, real and perceived risks, pressures, challenges, goals, objectives, vision, technical performance, schedule, cost.

Examples of customer concerns include the following:

- Budget constraints influencing implementation of the contract or completion of the buy.
- Increased demands by their internal customers (the actual product or service users) on their performance.
- Not meeting their internal customers' expectations.
- Ability to meet new product design requirements.
- Tighter schedules.
- Transition from the incumbent contractor to a new contractor.
- Anticipated and unanticipated issues surrounding program consolidations.
- Past challenges delivering products and services.
- Lack of existing contractor organizational flexibility.
- Challenges adapting to new processes, systems, or technology.
- Releasing control to contractors and trusting contractor results.
- Effective testing and quality control.
- Difficulty accurately estimating cost and schedule performance.

The customer's major concerns can typically be grouped into one or more of the following categories:

- Lowering cost.
- Increasing performance.
- Lowering risk.
- Increasing quality, reliability, and maintainability.
- Improving schedule and delivery.
- Facilitating graceful technology insertion over time without disruption to existing service.
- Increasing innovation.
- Improving the overall quality of the contractor's team.

Use Table 1.1 to document your customer's hot buttons, their potential effect on the procurement effort (management, technical, cost, and/or schedule), and your team's approach to addressing each item. When you prepare this list, don't worry about the number of hot buttons that are identified or from whom on the customer's side they originated. Capture all of them and then refine this list as you continue to better understand the customer and who the real decision makes are.

As communications with the customer continue over time, prioritize your list. Add or eliminate items from the list as you feel appropriate. The maturity of your list and the amount of time that you put into developing and vetting it with the customer will greatly impact the quality of your presentation, how it is received by the customer, and ultimately, the outcome of the procurement.

Always remember that the more you know about the customer and the procurement decision maker, the more capable you are of assuring them that you are the best team to address their concerns and challenges. Use your customer intelligence to tailor your presentation so you clearly

Table 1.1 Listing Customer Hot Buttons

Customer Hot Button	Potential Effect On Your Offering	Team Approach

demonstrate that your team knows, understands, and can operate in the customer's environment effectively, efficiently, and successfully.

Evaluation Criteria

Analyze Every Customer Need and Requirement—Study and Understand the Evaluation Criteria

To optimally respond to any solicitation, your team must thoroughly understand all the procurement documentation including the specifications, work tasks, and the evaluation criteria for the contract award. You must also understand any and all special directions or requirements that are frequently scattered throughout the procurement documents. Although these elements may overlap, they are not the same and may be interpreted differently depending on how and where they are presented in the solicitation.

Master's Tip: Ask Clarifying Questions, Don't Make Assumptions

Don't make any assumptions. It is only when your team double-checks all requirements to make sure every item is thoroughly addressed that you can be sure your proposal and presentation are fully compliant. Remember that at least one of the customers present during your presentation will be tasked to score the presentation by checking requirements to confirm compliance. If you have any questions whatsoever about the solicitation or what is required of you, ask the customer. It's never too late to ask!

As you prepare your presentation material, work to maximize your final evaluation score by ensuring that you address all major, and key minor, solicitation requirements. Use Table 1.2 to document the evaluation criteria in the solicitation and your team's response to each criterion.

Table 1.2   Matching Your Approach to Customer Evaluation Criteria

Customer's Evaluation Criteria	Team Approach

Master's Tip: Respond to Written Requirements, Don't Assume You Know "What the Customer Really Wants"

If you are the incumbent contractor, respond only to the RFP/ RFQ/PO requirements and avoid the biggest trap of all—assuming you know what the customer "really wants" versus what the written documentation actually asks for. Always remember that the customer's proposal and oral presentation evaluation team is guided by what's written in the solicitation and must evaluate your presentation using the requirements and contractual terms of the solicitation alone. In the case of US government procurements, it's the law!

Team Strengths and Weaknesses

Objectively Analyze Your Team's Strengths and Weaknesses
Relative to the Evaluation Criteria

You must objectively evaluate your team's strengths and weaknesses from the customer's perspective, and relative to the solicitation requirements and evaluation factors, in order to effectively leverage your strengths and mitigate your weaknesses.

List your team's strengths in Table 1.3.

Understanding how the customer, as well as competitors, perceivesyou strengthens your ability to address your weaknesses with approaches that improve your evaluation score and potentially weakens that of your competitors.

Whether your weaknesses are real or perceived, they are real in the eyes of the customer, and therefore pose a threat to your win probability if not addressed properly. Examples of common weaknesses include the following:

- Reputation of elitism or arrogance
- Personality conflicts with previous customers
- High turnover
- Complacency
- Excessively competitive nature
- Process stagnation
- Lack of flexibility
- Inappropriate communication
- Inability to protect confidential information
- Bad teaming reputation
- Defensive attitude
- "Incumbentitis"
- Unresponsive or overly rigid business model
- Expensive and/or known for post-award "cost growth"
- Not structurally aligned with customer
- Financial tracking/reporting challenges
- Poor marketing
- Disunity/infighting
- Inappropriately skilled personnel
- Poor internal communications
- Poor customer communication

Table 1.3 Listing Your Team's Strengths

Team Strengths

List your team's weaknesses (real and perceived) in Table 1.4.

Evaluate your team's strengths and weaknesses against the evaluation criteria in the solicitation. Strategize and develop approaches that will improve your scoring in each evaluated area. Use Tables 1.5 and 1.6 to help you document the results.

Competitor Strengths/Weaknesses

Analyze the Competing Teams' Strengths and Weaknesses Against the Evaluation Criteria

To position your team to win, you must understand the competition—who they are, how they operate, what their culture is like, what their strengths and weaknesses are, what successes they have had, and what failures they are currently experiencing or have experienced in the past. Keep in mind, as you are determining strategies to mitigate their strengths and expose their weaknesses, they are doing the same with respect to your team.

Table 1.4   Listing Your Team's Weaknesses

Team Weaknesses

Although it is essential to understand the competition, it is almost always counterproductive to specifically identify or call out their positive

Table 1.5 Leveraging Your Team's Strengths

Evaluation Criteria	Team Strength	Team Approach to Leverage

Table 1.6 Minimizing Your Team's Weaknesses

Evaluation Criteria	Team Weakness	Team Approach to Mitigate

or negative attributes in your proposal or oral presentation. "Ghosting" competition, which is essentially trying to discredit them in your presentation or proposal, is very tricky business that will be discussed later.

Document your competitive intelligence using Table 1.7. Complete one table for each competitor.

Master's Tip: Ensure That Your Team Is Knowledgeable and Current

Know your competition! Assembling a team of people with intimate, current knowledge of likely competitors to discuss their potential approach to the procurement is an essential ingredient for success. Draw upon people who have competed with potential competitors in the past, utilize individuals who have been reviously employed by the competition (but check with your legal counsel first to ensure there is no conflict of interest), and consider using consultants if they are current and not conflicted. Don't enlist the help of people who have dated information or are semi-knowledgeable. Using such people can do far more harm than good.

Remember that getting started early in the procurement process and working with the customer before "the door closes" may also provide valuable insight into the current contractor's performance. Do as much research into the competition as you can through open media and don't overlook any other non-proprietary sources of information you can find that may be helpful.

Sun Tzu in *The Art of War* wrote, "It is only the enlightened ruler and the wise general who will use the highest intelligence of the army for the purposes of spying, and thereby they achieve great results." Most definitely, spying is not being even remotely suggested here, but the solid principle of knowing your competition cannot be understated. Sun Tzu knew this in 512 B.C. and it has, without question, withstood the test of time!

Table 1.7 Evaluating the Competitor

Evaluation Criteria	Competitor Strength or Weakness	Team Approach to Counter Strength or Capitalize on Weakness

Presentation Win Strategy

Identify the Primary Elements of Your Approach That Strengthen Your Win Probability

Achieve Total Team Commitment to Success

Score High

Crush the Competition

A win strategy focuses your formal oral presentation on the most important factors and requirements of the solicitation. It must be both creative and compelling. It must also address every single customer hot button, using your prioritized list as a guide.

An effective win strategy has two parts: (1) It addresses the solicitation objectives, requirements, and customer hot buttons; (2) It describes your approach to achieving those objectives, requirements, and customer needs.

Your win strategy should be simple but creative, not too detailed, and easy for everyone to understand. As we all know, and have experienced in a variety of ways, simple solutions and strategies needed to conquer complex problems are hard to achieve. They require a great deal of thought and may take time to evolve. But when an exceptional strategy emerges, everyone intuitively knows it's the right one, and you will enjoy the tremendous advantage of having total team commitment to success. It will be obvious to all that the right strategy has been achieved. The answer will be elegant in its simplicity. It will be a winner!

To win, you must:

- Score high relative to the customer's evaluation criteria.
- Effectively lower the competitors' score by having a superior approach.
- Defend yourself against the competitors' efforts to reduce your score.
- Address all the customer's needs and requirements, but focus on a relatively small number of key points that your audience can and will remember.
- Most importantly, out-think and outwit the competition in every respect and ensure your presentation communicates your discriminators.

To begin to create your win strategy, use your customer, competitors, and team analysis to determine what it will take for your team to win. Document each "what" as an objective. When you have completed your "what" list, ask yourself and your team this question, "If we achieve every one of our objectives, will we win?" If the answer is yes, congratulate yourselves and move forward. If the answer is no, don't stop working your objectives until you get to the seemingly impossible yes. Don't give up; with the right team and participants you'll get there!

Examples of objectives might include the following:

- Convince the customer that your team offers a very low risk program.
- Objectively distance your team from the recognized primary competitor by highlighting the discriminators associated with your approach.
- Describe a plan showing that a transition from the incumbent contractor is beneficial to the customer and will be seamless/not disruptive to current program performance.

- Eliminate any potential customer concerns about your talent, skills, or management expertise.
- Demonstrate that your technical and management approach is superior to that of the competition.
- Show how you will credibly reduce cost and achieve all schedule and technical requirements with margin.

Brainstorm a list of your top three to five potential objectives—what it will take to win. Refer to the solicitation requirements and customer hot buttons frequently to guide you during this process. Prioritize and document the objectives using Table 1.8, limiting your list to no more than five. Next, you'll address a detailed strategy and approach for achieving each objective.

Determine how you will achieve each guiding objective and create distance between your team and the competition. For example:

- Convince the customer that your team offers the lowest program or project transition risk (objective) by showing how each element of your plan has been used to transition contracts of similar size and scope successfully in the past (approach).
- Eliminate the customer's concerns about your engineering expertise (objective) by conducting rigorous engineering trade studies on key technical attributes and then detailing your selected approach for each of the evaluator's issues or concerns (approach).
- Create distance between your team and the recognized primary competitor (objective) by demonstrating that your solution is more comprehensive and perfectly aligned with contractual and programmatic requirements (approach) versus alternate approaches. This is a very effective way of ghosting the competition without mentioning them by name.
- Demonstrate that your technical approach is superior and cost effective (objective) by including detailed analysis that shows how you will meet the requirements versus simply including unsubstantiated claims or "parroting back requirements" (approach).

Table 1.8 Creating a List of Objectives and How to Achieve Them

Guiding Objective	Approach

Document your approach to each objective in the Approach column of Table 1.8. Then you can combine the objectives and approaches from the columns to develop your win strategy.

Your win strategy will consist of statements you'll derive from combining each objective with its solution. When you document your win strategy, be careful not to substitute quantity for quality. Write down your three to five brief, focused win strategy statements, keep them in front of you, and apply them as you develop your formal presentation.

Master's Tip: Describe How You Will Satisfy Your Customer to Win Their Confidence

Telling "how" objectives and requirements will be satisfied greatly contributes to making your presentation convincing. It shows that you understand your customer's needs and demonstrates you know what must be done to satisfy their needs. The "how" part of any presentation or proposal might just be the hardest part! It takes a great deal of thought and an ability to articulate and document how you are going to get the job done. People who can convincingly answer "how" will win the customer's confidence. Simply parroting back requirements will annoy any customer. Take the time to think through every issue and determine how you will answer the inevitable question that every customer asks: "How are you going to do that?"

Value Proposition

Tell the Customer Why They Should Buy Your Solution
Demonstrate Tangible and Beneficial Results Associated with Your
Unique Value Proposition

A value proposition describes the primary reason the customer should select your offering rather than the competition's.

Your value proposition is your key message. Keep it simple. It must tell the customer the unique, credible, and quantifiable impact of your solution to assure them that they will achieve their goals and objectives. Your value proposition must include four key elements:

- **Tell *what* you are offering,** for example, people, product, process, service.
- **Explain *why and how* your offering helps them resolve their challenges,** for example, realize cost benefits; develop workforce; improve tasks, processes, efficiency, and/or internal/external customer satisfaction.
- **Quantify *how much* value the customer gains from implementing your solution,** for example, a 25% performance improvement = $X cost savings.
- **Demonstrate *where* you've had proven success with your solution,** for example, achievements from current or past on-contract work, prior metrics tracking and trending, verbatim customer praise. Consider offering a service, performance-based, or product warranty/guarantee if beneficial to do so.

Use this outline to begin documenting your value proposition:

1. What do you offer?
2. Why and how does your offer help the customer resolve a particular challenge?
3. How much will the customer gain from implementing your solution?

4. Where have you successfully implemented your solution, and what were the results?

Test potential value propositions against these criteria:

- Does it truly offer the best solution to meet the customer's needs?
- Does it answer what, why, and how much?
- Will the customer believe it?
- Does it differentiate your team?
- Is it stated in three to five simple points?
- Is it free of business jargon and marketing hype?
- Is it easy to understand in about five seconds?
- Are all claims substantiated with real data or rigorous analysis?

Your value proposition is your overall theme for your proposal and for your oral presentation. It guides everything that goes into your presentation. Post it and memorize it. Make sure you know how it affects your presentation.

Win Themes and Discriminators

Show How You Outshine the Competition!

Discriminators are unique attributes that truly differentiate your offering from those of your competitors. They are the special or unusual capabilities that you can offer in your presentation, including evidence of their successful use to legitimize your claim that you are uniquely and optimally qualified to do the job. The extent to which your discriminators align with the customer's formal/informal buying criteria, and successfully address all evaluation factors, significantly contributes to your win probability.

Here are a few examples of true discriminators:

- A patent or copyright that enables only you to offer the benefits of utilizing it.

- A special procedure or process that is proprietary to you or your company.
- An approach to solving a problem that has never been done before.
- New methodologies, implementation of existing technology in a new or unique way, or introduction of new technology.
- An investment that is made as a part of your offer.
  - Utilization of people with special skills or experience.
  - Independent research and development effort or capitalizing upon similar projects or developments that are applicable to your offering.
  - Funding activities associated with program transition from an incumbent at no cost to the customer.
  - Funding special projects at no cost to the customer following award that enhance project performance (technical, cost, schedule) in any way.
- Creative management approaches that have not previously been used.

Master's Tip: Credibility Skyrockets When You Justify and Quantify Your Claims

Whenever you can convincingly quantify the impact of your value proposition, your credibility skyrockets in the eyes of the customer. Any time and energy that you spend to quantify the value prop impact will be well worth it because doing so:

1. Shows you understand the customer's issues.

2. Provides your customers with valuable information they may not have themselves.

3. Demonstrates you are committed to helping your customers solve their most pressing issues.

To ensure that you do not defocus your presentation team, consider assigning a special task team to do the analysis and provide you with the needed information. Off-loading this task to a group of smart people keeps the presentation team focused and puts the right minds on the analysis task.

If a written proposal has already been submitted, hopefully the value prop analysis is included in that document and you can use it to your advantage. If not included in the written proposal, and time permits, get it done!

Your early preparation work analyzing the customer's requirements/criteria establishes the foundation for identifying your discriminators. Ideally your team's solution will meet or exceed all evaluation criteria including areas where the competition is weak.

Discriminators express a positive selling point for your team and objectively separate you from the competition. They are derived from:

- Your knowledge of the customer and competitors.
- Your understanding of the solicitation requirements and evaluation criteria.
- The creativity and uniqueness of your approach.
- Your team's performance, both past and present.
- Your team's reputation with the customer and within the industry.
- Your employees and their accomplishments.
- Your resources, including potential investments.

To help you identify your team's discriminators, address and answer the following:

- What components and elements of our approach are truly unique?
- What are our key points?

- When teaming or subcontracting is required, do we demonstrate an optimized, well managed, organized team? How? Have teammates, subcontractors, and vendors previously worked together successfully with us?
- Do we answer the customer's "what," "how," and "so what"?
- Do we project and substantiate credibility?
- Finally, of paramount importance, will customers understand how our discriminators benefit them, and do they value them?

Master's Tip: Discriminators Must Be Truly Unique to Boost You Above Your Competition

Elements of your solution that are not truly unique are not discriminators. Claiming, or puffing up, something that is not truly a discriminator can actually hurt you in the evaluation and selection process. In the context of a discriminator, making misconceived or inflated claims shows you don't understand the real issues at hand. Don't fall into this trap. Ensure that your discriminators are genuine and are recognized by customers as bringing real, unique value to the project.

Ideally, early in the proposal preparation process, vet what you believe to be your discriminators with your customers. Most customers will tell you what they think about your ideas and your approach; it's human nature to do so. Know that your discriminators are real and that customers believe that they are real too. Clearly, this is a real plus when it comes time to write your proposal and make your presentation!

Past discriminators may not necessarily be applicable in the current environment. Over time, customer preferences and approaches, industry and technology trends, and your team's capabilities grow and change. Discriminators must be continuously reassessed to ensure your claims are accurate, applicable, and current.

A few hard-hitting, concrete discriminators are far better than a larger number of them, some of which may be questionable in the mind of the customer. Remember the somewhat overused, but wise, old adage, *If it sounds too good to be true, it probably is.*

Take time to think through your win strategy thoroughly, keeping in mind that the real discriminators are the ones that drive your approach and separate you from your competition. Feature your winning discriminators, ensure they are cornerstones of your presentation, and be confident they will resonate with your customer.

Your team discriminators represent your key selling points. Your win themes support and reinforce your discriminators within specific sections of your oral presentation. Theme statements should be included/referenced as frequently as possible without being overbearing or annoying.

Examples of potential win themes, each of which must be supported with relevant, specific, quantified data, include the following:

- We have delivered similar (examples of products/services) with (documented or audited), industry leading results in ... (examples).
- We have a cost-effective approach that improves performance (how much) and minimizes risk (how).
- We have designed a scalable solution for your program that is easily, seamlessly, and cost-effectively expanded to accommodate future growth (show how and how much money is saved).
- We have executed similar, low-risk program transitions from incumbents (give successful examples that the referenced customer will agree with).
- We have selected and optimized features to meet your specific needs and requirements: innovation, stability, corporate reach back, corporate and subcontractor/supplier support, etc. (describe each element; always quantify).
- We are able to offer exceptional warranties and leverage proven experience, solutions, and processes that will greatly reduce implementation risk on this program (what and how).

- We have a positive working relationship with (individual/organization/element). Show how that knowledge or relationship relates to this contract.

Use Table 1.9 to ensure that pertinent sections of your orals presentation include the appropriate win themes and discriminators. Make sure you don't overlook talking about your key win themes and discriminators. And yes, unfortunately that can and does happen!

Table 1.9 Listing Themes and Discriminators

Orals Section	Win Theme	Discriminator

Master's Tip: Getting to "Blue" Is Tough Work, but It's Winning Work

Getting to blue is no easy task. It requires a thorough understanding of many elements that, by definition, are tightly interwoven and dependent on each other. It requires: strategic thinking to formulate your approach, technical expertise, management excellence, customer mission understanding, cost management, and intimate knowledge of the competitive field. Thorough preparation, thinking through every issue, an unwavering commitment to win, and planning are essential ingredients of a "blue" presentation.

Once you feel that you have all of the essential elements of a winning proposal/presentation prepared and documented, bring in the experts and discuss your approach with them before you move to the next step. Experts are trusted individuals who are familiar with the customer, the procurement, your capabilities, and the competition. They are smart, experienced people who have not been intimately involved in helping you develop your win strategy. Use them to objectively assess your strategy, point out the strengths and weakness of your approach, make constructive suggestions for improvement, and perform an overall assessment of your ability to win the job.

A robust discussion is always best, so encourage your reviewers to speak their minds. Silence is a valuable ally; allow the customer to give you their complete, uninterrupted feedback while you attentively acknowledge it and take notes. Don't be defensive, be open-minded, and give thoughtful consideration to all suggestions for improvement.

Getting to Blue!

Take Time and Carefully Think Through Every Issue!

The color blue is actually used by a number of buyers in US government procurement. It represents the highest possible score that can be obtained and states that, "the offeror demonstrates a clear and detailed understanding of all aspects of the work to be performed." So when we say, "Let's get to blue," it's essentially saying, "Let's get to a perfect proposal" or realistically, one that's darn near perfect!

Your team's goal is to achieve a "blue" rating. Here is a concise checklist of must-haves that will facilitate your team's ability to build a successful presentation and "go blue."

- Know your customer.
- Know your competition.
- Thoroughly understand your win strategy and know that it is valid.
- Know your value proposition and be able to articulate it.
- Capitalize on key win themes and discriminators.
- Use a compliance matrix (to ensure that all requirements are satisfied).
- List all risks and associated risk mitigators.
- Develop a schedule of events leading up to the formal presentation.
- Ensure that all presentation charts have brief, clearly understood titles (define "what") and takeaways (answer the question, "so what?").

Chapter 2

Secrets of Successful Presenters

An Audience Quickly Forgets the Ordinary—Don't Be Ordinary!

S uccessful presenters do indeed have secrets that they use very effectively. They are powerful concepts that should be considered, re-considered, reviewed, and re-reviewed as you prepare your presentation.

The customer will attend as many presentations as there are companies competing for the work. Typical presentations with typical graphics and traditional presenters secure at best an "average" or "mediocre" position. This is not good enough to win! You must do something different to make the customer remember your team, while still meeting all of the requirements.

The following techniques will help make your presentation memorable. They are easy to understand and hard to implement, so keep them in front of you from the first moment you begin planning your presentation until the day of delivery to your customer.

Let Your "Self" Shine Through

Your Strength as a Speaker Comes from Within

Great speakers connect with their audience. The connection comes not only from a shared interest in the subject matter, but also from the speaker's personal interest and passion for the topic. You cannot inspire or persuade anyone to do something unless you are inspired and convinced yourself. You must believe in what you are presenting and you must show the customer how dedicated you are to the solution you are offering.

A wise person once said that the most important thing in life is to enjoy your work, to find your passion and pursue it with vigor. Think about that. You pursued your job for a reason, and you go back each day for a reason. Recall and build on your original enthusiasm for your job and translate that into enthusiasm for the subject matter you are presenting.

Sincere passion is contagious and inspiring. Great leaders are passionate about their goals and their teams. They express that passion in a way that other people can identify with, and as a result, people follow. Successful companies have passionate leaders who grab investors' attention, attract top talent, and perform with excellence in every way.

Your passion and enthusiasm infect the customer with positive feelings toward you, and by extension, your team and your offering. Find your passion and let it shine through. Your strength as a speaker comes from within.

Document your passion for this opportunity. Ask yourself and your team the following questions:

1. What are you passionate about?
2. Why were you first interested in pursuing this opportunity?
3. Which portions of your topic and our overall approach are you most passionate about? Why?

The Power of Personal Stories

Personal Stories Enhance Credibility and Demonstrate That You Truly Understand What the Real Issues Are

Stories create a connection with the audience. They add tremendous credibility to your presentation when they are genuine, applicable to your subject, and evoke an emotional response. Stories illustrate, clarify, and inspire. They bring real-world experience for which we all know there is no substitute.

For example, while preparing an oral presentation to perform quality assurance work for NASA, each speaker was asked to include a personal story in their presentation that demonstrated their passion for the work. The proposed deputy program manager included the following paraphrased story.

> As a young adult I lived in Florida in the 1980s, and got as much of a thrill from watching a launch as I did from walking on the beach at sunrise. One morning in early 1986 as I was walking along the beach marveling at the sunrise, I happened to look down, and my mood changed instantly. I bent over and picked up a debris fragment from the Space Shuttle *Challenger* disaster. At that moment I swore I would do anything I could to prevent such a disaster from ever happening again—and now I have my chance.

What was said in the rest of this person's presentation didn't matter. The customers were already convinced that this individual was someone they wanted to work with. In the debriefing from the customer after this team won the job, the customer stated that most of the competing teams gave good presentations, but this team's presentation was exceptional and memorable. They were selected because they connected with their audience.

Master's Tip: Personal Stories That the Customer Identifies with Are Powerful and Greatly Enhance Your Credibility

Personal stories can be very powerful, but be absolutely certain that your story relates solidly with the customer and the issue they are facing. When a connection is made via a relevant story, a special relationship is made with the customer.

"This person really gets it" is the desired effect you want to have on your audience. Conversely, not relating to the customer with a personal story can have a detrimental effect and result in a negative "so what" reaction.

To ensure that stories are relevant, test them on your team early in the preparation process and insist on brutally candid feedback. If the story is powerful and works well—great, use it! If it's weak or not totally relevant, scrap it. Don't try to twist the story, puff it up, or sugarcoat it. It's better to omit a personal story altogether than to use one that can potentially alienate your audience or negatively impact your credibility.

There are three types of stories that may have a significant impact on your presentation:

1. Personal stories.
2. Stories about other people's experiences.
3. Stories that illustrate how your solution is perfectly suited to meet the customer's needs.

Stories humanize you, your team, and your company. They go a long way toward addressing one of the customer's goals for requiring presentations: to determine whether they want to work with your team. Passionate people, an optimal solution, and real stories related to the customer's needs are a winning combination.

Document your potential stories and screen them by asking the following questions.

1. What personal experience shows your passion for this opportunity and this customer?
2. What experience of someone else demonstrates the passion you share for this opportunity and this customer?
3. How does this story demonstrate why your solution is exceptional?

Converse Rather Than Lecture

No One Wants to Be Lectured at; Converse with Your Audience to Hold Their Attention

Practice until you internalize your content and can deliver it as comfortably as having a conversation with a friend. Your goal is not to lecture your audience, but rather to converse with the audience in a natural conversational tone at a normal rate of speech. An authentic presentation requires hours of work to: (a) choose the exact words that best represent your passion for your subject and (b) hone your ability to deliver those words with maximum impact.

Maximum impact is achieved when both your verbal and nonverbal communication skills are optimized. Practice out loud in front of a mirror using hand gestures that come naturally to you. Early in the planning process, video record yourself delivering your presentation and use it to determine how to make your presentation better. Video record yourself again close to the formal presentation date to see how much you've improved.

Practice in front of your team, watch for their reaction, and get their feedback. Practice in front of people who haven't been a part of the preparation process to see how they react. Passion for your topic combined with practice creates the presence you need to deliver your best performance.

Master's Tip: Bring in Wise Trusted Outsiders to Critique Your Approach and Your Presentation

When you feel you have your presentation close to being finalized, bring in trusted outsiders to critique it. Be careful whom you select for your reviewers. Make sure that your reviewers read all of the solicitation requirements and have received a thorough briefing about the customer and the competition. Ideally those selected will know, or will have worked with, the customer in the past. Optimally they will have actually been the customer in the past and have professionally moved on by joining your organization or becoming a consultant. They should be people who are exceptionally insightful, thoughtful, and smart.

Ultimately, formal dress rehearsals will be conducted to polish the final product, but getting an early start and constructive, meaningful feedback will save you valuable time by reducing rework and a significant amount of stress!

Teach the Customer Something They Don't Already Know

Prevent Audience Boredom—Present New and Exciting Information That Creatively Addresses Your Customer's Needs

The customer will probably watch several presentations on the same subject matter. Your job is to present information about your offering that is completely new, packaged differently, or offers a new way to solve a problem or challenge in their environment. Find a way to present new and exciting information.

Most college professors are passionate about their subject matter, yet some students fall asleep during lectures. Thought-provoking professors recognize that their topic may not be as exciting to their students as it is to them and use techniques to create images, thoughts, and facts that stick in students' minds. You may know the basics of the subject, but presenting it from a different perspective, or in a different way, makes it fresh and new.

Your job is to present information, with which the customer may be painstakingly familiar, in a way that makes your team memorable. Apple Inc. does this well. They sell computers and smartphones, as do many other manufacturers, yet Apple stirs public curiosity and interest year after year, with products designed to excite us and make us look forward to their next-generation offerings. Apple advertising doesn't emphasize technical features such as RAM/ROM or pixels in their screen technology. They show you how their products will change your life, and indeed, Apple and others like them have changed our lives. The technology itself is life changing, not solely because of the technical details behind their products, but because of what it can do for you.

Your customer is looking for new ways to solve their problems too. You have interesting anecdotes and experiences that are valuable for presenting your material from a different and memorable perspective. Identify and bring out these features; use them to your advantage.

If you didn't believe in the unique value of your offering, you wouldn't be competing for the work. Explore the original passion that resulted in the decision to pursue this opportunity. Explore your own unique passion for your subject. Present something new and novel to the customer, or show them your solution from a different perspective. Give them a new and different way to solve their problems and paint a mental picture of how much better everything will be for them when they select you. Most speakers are more creative than they give themselves credit for. Tap into that creativity, and harness it to produce a winning presentation.

Document what the customer doesn't already know about your solution.

1. What is truly unique about your solution, that is, what are your discriminators?
2. Why are you passionate about your solution?
3. Describe your solution with enthusiasm.
4. Paint a mental picture for the customer of how your solution will make their lives better.

Include Something Astounding

Everyone Likes to Be Pleasantly Surprised—Work Hard to Find and Present Something New and Exciting

Somewhere in your presentation, deliver something shocking or surprising. It should be so amazing that it instantly grabs the audience's attention. It should create an emotional reaction in the customer's mind that makes it easy to remember in spite of the time they will sit listening to each and every team's presentation.

We all remember astounding moments in our lives, such as winning an award, making a difference in someone's life, solving a particularly difficult problem, or achieving something we never thought we would. Including astounding moments in your presentation will make a lasting impression on the audience and differentiate you from other competitors.

Master's Tip: Immediately Capture Your Audience's Attention and Make Them Want to Hear More

Winning presentations and speeches start by capturing the audience's attention immediately. No one wants to listen to a boring presentation that drones on and on. Your goal is to capture your audience's attention and keep them intrigued and excited about what is yet to come. Make them want to hear more! This technique requires much thought and considerable skill in delivery. A strong start is essential; without it, recovery is very difficult.

It is akin to the fine art of stand-up comedy. Wit, impeccable timing, and content (read this as your discriminators, approach, and win theme) are crucial.

Preparation is everything and the tasks described in Chapter 1 are prerequisites and essential ingredients in every winning presentation.

Statistics can be boring, or, conversely, they can make your jaw drop. Consider Apple's introduction of the iPod in 2001 when their major competition was basically the cassette tape–based Sony Walkman. You could have described the iPod's size (very thin, very small, very light, plays music) or you could tell the story of how you interact with it (smaller than a deck of cards, enables you to carry thousands of your favorite songs in your pocket or purse and play them all day long without changing or recharging batteries or messing with tapes).

Which statistics are more intriguing? Clearly we know the one that Apple selected! Fact: About three billion iPods were sold in the first 16 years since its introduction, with sales still continuing despite smartphones taking their place. Not bad, not bad at all! And, don't forget the revolutionary and incredibly successful storefront it also created ... iTunes. Astounding, exceptionally profitable, and enduring? You bet!

Put your data and information into a context that matters to the customer. How will it make their lives better and satisfy their needs? Why is it vital for the future? How much impact will it have on their challenges or their environment?

As you move forward with preparing your presentation content, keep in mind that your customer's response is not necessarily created from the facts of your presentation, but rather in how you present them. You can create astounding and memorable moments with stories, quotes, graphics, and videos that describe your solution.

For example, as you prepare your win strategy, win themes, and discriminators, be thinking about high-impact titles and takeaways that will represent the main point of each chart in your presentation. What's the one fact you want the evaluators to remember from the chart even if they forget everything else? Are they more likely to remember "Our Organizational Structure Fosters Open Communication" or "Our Team Is Co-Located with Your Organization to Ensure Open Communication"?

Consider including memorable quotes, photographs, illustrations, or videos in your presentation. Including unique, positive customer quotes about your performance on other programs is also very powerful. Photographs of people they recognize implementing your solution add credibility and help you connect with the evaluators and decision-makers.

To test the impact of quotes, videos, and images, practice your delivery in front of a new audience and at the end ask them what they remember about your presentation. You can do this as part of both individual practice and the end-to-end dress rehearsal. The more feedback you solicit from qualified individuals, the more powerful you can make your presentation.

Make your presentation memorable by following these steps:

1. Describe and quantify how and why your solution is the best.
2. Describe and quantify why your solution is beneficial to the customer. What positive impact will it have?
3. Document metrics, quotes, and stories that demonstrate how and why your solution is the best.
4. Develop memorable phrases (sound bites, potential chart titles/takeaways) that emphasize your responses to the first three questions.
5. Select photos, graphics, illustrations, and videos that help to communicate your points and your approach in a meaningful way.

Keep It Short, Sweet, and Direct

Get to the Point Quickly to Create a Memorable Impression

The average adult attention span is 20 minutes, and listening intently for long periods of time is draining. Your team's entire presentation will likely take significantly longer than 20 minutes, but use the 20-minute rule to plan each speaker's section. Include handing off to the next speaker within 20 minutes whenever you can.

Incorporating a mental break (a story, new perspective, astounding element) into each section not only makes your presentation memorable, it also makes the customer look forward to the next section to hear another story, a new perspective, or astounding element.

You know a great deal about your topic, or you wouldn't have been selected as a presenter. Your goal is not to present everything you know about your topic, but rather to convey the most important content in a meaningful and memorable way.

Our brains are wired to retain three to seven items in short-term memory, which is why speakers frequently talk about three key items. Three points are easy to remember. The more you include, the more brainpower your audience needs to expend to absorb your material.

Attempt to keep the primary points in each section to not more than seven. And, if you use seven, try to use your mental break somewhere in the middle of your presentation to ensure that you retain the audience's attention. Your ultimate goal is to make it easy to select you as the winner.

It's harder to make a point, or present a topic, in fewer words versus many words. However, presenting a point with fewer, more memorable words helps you achieve your goal better than a long-winded explanation does. Support your chart title with as few primary points as possible, then provide supporting evidence as succinctly as possible.

Repetition may be the mother of learning, but after an evaluator has heard nearly the same thing three times or more, that evaluator is longing for something new and different. Don't dull your point with too many words, or with too much repetition.

Keep these secrets of successful presenters in mind as you use the remainder of this book for specific, in-depth guidance, techniques, and suggestions on how to make your presentation or speech memorable and powerful.

Chapter 3

Presentation and Messaging Preparation

Key Elements to Increase Your Win Probability

Your preparation work defines: (1) the key messages that you want the customer to understand and remember; (2) the competitive environment; (3) the customer's environment; (4) the customer's formal and informal buying criteria. These elements and the impact they have on your winning strategy must be reflected in both the formal presentation documentation and the accompanying script. As you prepare your formal documents, use your preparation work to evaluate the effectiveness of your presentation.

Your presentation should focus on five major messages:

1. We understand this job (show them) and we want to be your contractor/supplier.
2. We've done it, or very similar things, before (give examples).

3. Here's how we will do it for you (show them).
4. Here's how our approach benefits you (improved management, technical performance, cost, schedule, risk, quality).
5. Here's why our approach is best (trade studies, comparisons, discriminators, ghosting, indirect messaging).

Select Content

If It Doesn't Help You Win, Don't Include It!

As you select content, focus on the items of the most interest to the customer. Be emphatic and try to put yourself in your customer's position. Make sure your content completely and effectively addresses the following core elements that the customer will be looking for:

- **People.** Is this team the one that I prefer to work with? Do they exude integrity? Can I trust them? Are they passionate about my mission?
- **Capability.** Does this team offer the most effective and efficient solutions to my challenges? Do the solutions lower my risk, increase quality and reliability, improve technical and schedule performance, and deliver or offer appropriate innovation? Why would I want their solutions and how will they help me?
- **Experience.** Has this team successfully implemented similar solutions for similar customers? Am I their guinea pig for unproven and risky approaches?
- **Qualifications.** Do the team members have the required qualifications including certifications, education, security clearances, special capabilities, and required years of experience? Do subcontractors and vendors add value to the team?
- **Cost.** Does this team's cost align with their offering? Can I afford them? Are they worth it? Have they provided cost-effective

management and staffing solutions? Are they low-balling the price just to win the job and will this create a problem for me later?

- **Technical.** Does the proposed technical solution meet all my requirements? Does the technical solution exceed requirements in a way that is beneficial to me without adding cost? Does the proposed technical solution reduce risk?
- **Schedule.** Does the proposal meet all my schedule needs? Does it meet my needs sooner than required in a beneficial way?

Align these core elements with your preparation work to help determine the most essential content. Revisit, review, and align:

- Customer intelligence, its potential effect on this procurement, and your team's approach to addressing it.
- Evaluation criteria.
- Win themes and discriminators.
- Key messages.
- Your team's approach to leveraging strengths and mitigating weaknesses, as well as ghosting competitors.
- Incorporate additional information from this exercise to align your preparation work with the core elements. Use a compliance matrix to make sure you remain compliant with the solicitation and cover all major requirements.

As you select your content for each section of the presentation, stay focused on your overall value proposition and win strategy. Determine three to seven major points for the section that address your customer's pertinent priorities (use a copy of Table 3.1 for each section). Link these to your overall value proposition, win strategy, discriminators, and key elements/messages in order to convince the customer to award your team the contract. Major points must be stated clearly and simply.

Table 3.1 Focusing Your Points on the Customer's Priorities

Major Points	Capability, Experience, and Qualifications	Win Themes and Discriminators
[Major Point]	[Key section elements and messages]	[Key section themes and discriminators]

Using your preparation work, create an outline of your presentation. Ensure you address all evaluation criteria, the core elements of interest to the customer, your win themes, differentiators, and key messages. Use your outline to help determine what to include as primary and backup material.

As you develop and finalize content, make sure you:

- Address the customer's formal and informal buying criteria.
- Avoid presenting interesting data about yourself or your company if it does not help you win.
- Anticipate their questions and answer them during your presentation.
- Demonstrate your familiarity with their systems, processes, requirements, business culture, traditions, pressures, internal/external customers, and any other relevant areas.

- Find ways to reduce verbiage with impactful graphics, video, and photos.
- Align your vision and your content with the customer's expectations; not too narrow or too broad.
- Include clear, concise information describing how you will implement your solutions and why they benefit the customer.
- Select content that will emphasize any cost or risk reduction, increased production efficiencies, improved quality and performance, or enhanced schedule. Be as specific as possible, and quantify the savings your solutions will provide.
- Include and highlight awards, customer and industry recognition, and performance scores (collectively and individually). When teaming or subcontracting, don't assume that the customer is familiar with the companies and vendors you have selected. Explain their roles on the project and why you selected them to be members of your team.
- Consider using a short story or an example to illustrate your point.
- Use specific examples to emphasize that you are fully compliant with all requirements.
- Fully support your examples with data that is real and relevant, such as qualitatively and/or quantitatively verifiable information to which the customer can relate. Include previous customer recognition if possible.
- Demonstrate that communication is vital to the effectiveness and health of the contract and success of the customer's mission. Include a chart that shows regular, one-on-one communication with the counterparts in each group: customer and contractor.
- Avoid the temptation to spend too much time on what you have done in the past instead of focusing on what you will do during this contract's period of performance.
- Omit extraneous material that will dull your key messages. Every item, concept, claim, fact, experience, tool, skill, capability, talent, and strength must be significant.

- Review your content against these essential questions:
  - Does it address your real purpose?
  - Does it emphasize your key points?
  - Will you demonstrate a united team?
  - Do you provide a unique capability? How?
  - Do you answer their "so what?"
  - Will you project credibility?
  - Will the customer understand and appreciate your material?

Have an independent person verify that your raw content addresses the key requirements and evaluation criteria.

An additional issue regarding content is obvious but will create havoc if overlooked. Ensure that everyone on your team who is preparing content is held to a schedule, knows which topics and specific items they are responsible for, and gets their work done on time.

If for some reason an individual cannot meet these requirements, replace that person immediately. There is no time for compromise when preparing an oral presentation.

Replacement can be a difficult decision to make; however, your success depends on it. Total dedication to the orals process must be a mandate if you expect to have a winning presentation. Failure to dedicate people to this task will result in a mediocre presentation at best. Ask yourself when a mediocre performance was ever good enough to win anything!

Generating a written proposal requires a process, and so does pulling together a winning oral presentation. The written proposal is largely systematic, much like that of a factory production line. Conversely, creating a winning oral presentation is like composing a symphony: creativity, harmony, and synchronization are all essential ingredients. And, for a symphony to be complete, every member of the orchestra must be present and play their very best.

Master's Tip: If You Believe It's "Yours to Lose", You Will (Lose, That Is).

Incumbents beware! If you are an incumbent contractor you must avoid the following common, often overlooked, pitfalls:

- **Pitfall:** Assuming past performance is all-important and what you have done in the past will assure you of a future win.
  - **Truth:** Customers care much more about what you will do for them in the future!
  - **Truth:** The past is interesting, but not necessarily pertinent.
- **Pitfall:** Thinking that you know "what the customer really wants" versus what's described and asked for in the solicitation.
  - **Truth:** This will frequently lead to a solution that is either far more than the customer is asking for (exceeds requirements and is probably more expensive) or one that falls short of expectations (does not meet minimum requirements).
- **Pitfall:** Assuming that keeping the old incumbent team together is the right thing to do because it's performed and worked well in the past.
  - **Truth:** Frequently the old team is no longer the right team.
- **Pitfall:** Not thoroughly addressing all solicitation requirements and blissfully relying on past performance.
  - **Truth:** The past is not necessarily a reliable indicator of the future.
- **Pitfall:** Conveying a trust-me attitude.
  - **Truth:** No one likes arrogance.
- **Pitfall:** Not doing trade studies on new and different approaches since the current approach is working fine.
  - **Truth:** Complacency can be a deal-killer, and frequently it is.
- **And the biggest pitfall of all,** embracing an attitude that "It's ours to lose."
  - **Truth:** If you think it's yours to lose, you surely will!

Prepare Content for Delivery

Stories Have Far Greater Impact Than Statistics (But Pertinent and Persuasive Statistics Are Good Too)

The success of your presentation is in direct proportion to the effort you put into preparing it. The content of your presentation must be flawless: it forms the foundation of the customer's opinion of you and your team.

If your written proposal has been submitted earlier, the oral presentation is your opportunity to correct, modify, or enhance it based on your continuous learning about the customer and the competition. It is a unique opportunity to connect with the customer in a manner that makes them want to work with you more than with any other team. It's an additional chance to address both formal and informal buying criteria.

Everything you include in your graphics and script must positively and unequivocally answer the questions the customer is always consciously or subconsciously asking:

- "What's in it for us?"
- "How will you help us meet our objectives?"
- "Do you satisfy our needs and concerns?"
- "Do we want to work with you?"

To connect with your audience, use the following as a general guide and template in preparing your presentation:

- Get the customer's attention.
- Maintain their interest.
- Tell your story.
- Create a customer desire to work with your team by using logic, facts, examples, your plan, and your story.

Any piece of data, claim, or assertion you present must be translated to show how it will:

- Increase or maintain performance.
- Decrease risk.

- Decrease cost.
- Increase quality and reliability.
- Improve schedule and delivery.

Each element of your presentation requires energy and conviction from you. Use your knowledge of the customer to help ensure they will understand your presentation. Make sure all your anecdotes, stories, illustrations, examples, graphs, and data are true and compliant, compelling, cost-effective, and uniquely competitive, and that you energetically project competence, commitment, and credibility.

To avoid confusion and excessive rework, keep the content of the presentation under revision control following the first formal external team review or critique of the presentation. Government contractors generally refer to this first formal review as a "Pink Team" review.

At this point, changes should be made under the guidance and control of the team leader and with full participation of all presentation team members. It's important that the entire team participate in making changes: a change that may appear small to some may have a large impact on others. Continuity and a seamless flow across the entire presentation is vital, so don't overlook or downplay the importance of revision control.

Effective Graphics and Visuals—There Will Not Be a Second Opportunity to Create a Great First Impression

Charts and visuals help to form the all-important first impression and can enhance your win probability. They are also a potential pitfall.

Charts and visuals should lead your audience toward your team and your message, and they should complement your script. Before preparing graphics and visuals, revisit your goals and objectives. Be absolutely certain of the content and purpose of all elements of your presentation material and data. Make sure your team shares a common vision that will cohesively drive the look and feel of your presentation.

Use a template to ensure all charts have a consistent appearance (background color, font type and color, etc.). Format consistency equates to a high degree of professionalism and preparedness. Ensure the content of each chart supports and reinforces the other charts and that none of the information is contradictory.

Keep a uniform style and look across all graphics. Be consistent with bullets and flow. Make it easy for the customer to comprehend the intended message without being distracted by appearance inconsistencies.

Ensure the content is error free, including spelling. Typographical errors and conflicting data do not convey a sense of professionalism or attention to detail; they are unsettling and raise doubt in the mind of the customer.

Not everything you want to convey lends itself well to visual display, so don't force meaningless graphics. And don't use clip art or cartoons! This is unprofessional and shows you haven't taken the time to develop original graphics that specifically address your unique value proposition for your customer.

Generate your own meaningful graphics and ensure they are clear, easy to read, and support your key points. Accompanying script will supplement your charts and graphics and convey additional messaging that may not be possible to clearly express graphically.

Master's Tip: Present Your Key Message Quickly

Always begin each chart with your most important and impactful statement, and then ensure the rest of your chart supports this statement. The reason for doing this is that the majority of the audience will be paying the most attention each time a new chart is initially projected. Each individual in the audience will be looking for value and determining what their individual interest is in what you have to say. Literally seconds after the new chart comes up, you will either hold the majority of the audience's attention interest or lose it almost completely. Don't miss the opportunity to get your key message across to the entire audience—do it immediately, do it with enthusiasm, and build on the interest and energy it creates!

The following approach to content preparation (based on your presentation outline) helps ensure compliant, complete, and compelling material:

- **Give the "what."** This starts with the title of the chart, tells the customer what to expect, and defines the content of the chart. After the title, use content to demonstrate that you clearly understand the requirements and your approach to satisfying them.
- **Give the "how."** Provide details on how you will accomplish the "what."
- **Give the "so what."** Demonstrate how your approach will benefit the customer and create a win-win situation for all parties (your customer, you, your subcontractors, and your vendors). This can be reinforced with takeaways on your charts that succinctly state the benefits in the chart's content.
- **Give the "why."** Why is your approach superior to other options (be sure to substantiate with objective trade studies), or other competitors' solutions?

Master's Tip: The Art of Telling "How" Almost Always Separates Winners from Losers

The importance of "how" cannot be overstated. Without a convincing description and applicable supporting data, your claims remain unsubstantiated and may be questionable in the minds of customers. Frequently this element of a presentation is ignored and there can be a tendency to believe or assume that the "how" is obvious to customers. Never make this mistake. When it comes to "how," be thorough, be clear, and be concise. Also be sure to ask if there are any questions before moving on to the next topic. Spend lots of time on "how"!

Running a close second to "how" in terms of importance is "why." Once again, it's easy to assume that why you are taking a given approach, and why it's superior, is obvious to all. Making this assumption is a grave error. Why you have selected your approach must be convincing and substantiated. Trade studies, demonstrations, and tests are all excellent ways to justify your solution and provide meaningful information to your customer. This is also an excellent way to discredit your competition's approach without attacking them directly by name. Trade studies provide logical outcomes and virtually eliminate the need to single out any given competitor by name.

Remember, your competition is working hard for a win too. You may think you know exactly what they are proposing, but chances are quite good that you really don't! Never ever assume that you know exactly what a competitor's approach is. Rather, do the hard work that good trade studies require and base your approach on the outcome that best resonates with, and satisfies, your customer's needs. Your customers will thank you for this because it also helps them with the selection process!

Consider using a question and answer format for a few charts. Start the chart with a question, and then answer that question in the content of the chart. End the chart with a takeaway showing the benefit to the customer.

When selecting any item for a chart, make sure it meets the following tests:

- Is it informative?
- Is it foolproof or could it be misinterpreted?
- Is it necessary to accomplish your goals and objectives?
- Is it relevant to your messaging and to the customer?
- Does it justify the time and space it takes?

Effective graphics help customers visualize and focus on your team's strengths and ability to meet their needs. There are several basic tactics to remember as you develop your charts to help you create and maintain this focus. Understand these attributes and utilize the appropriate tactics to design charts that are clear and easy to understand:

- Traditionally, the eye travels from left to right, top to bottom, and clockwise.
- Colorblindness or color deficiency affects about 5% to 8% of males and less than 1% of females.
  - There are two major types of colorblindness: difficulty distinguishing between red and green, and difficulty distinguishing between blue and yellow.
  - To enhance readability, it is considered a best practice to use bright colors. People who have color deficiencies do see colors but they have a problem differentiating between them so using bright, bold colors helps.
  - Another issue to consider is the contrast between font and line colors and the background. People with color deficiencies are less sensitive to colors on either end of the spectrum (obviously, black and white being the most extreme). For example, reds and blues often appear to be darker to the color-deficient reader.
  - When preparing your chart template, test it out on someone who's color deficient before going into full chart production. Optimize your charts to meet their needs.
- Be more creative than simply listing content using bullets. Demonstrate concepts and explain them in your script, rather than including too much verbiage on your chart.
- There should never be any appearance of boilerplate text, cartoons, or "clip art."
- Use callouts on your charts to bring attention to key points you want to emphasize. Use shadow boxes, special colors or shapes, eye-catching words or designs in the callouts.
- Get permission to use any copyrighted material and give credit for it.

- Make sure your artwork clarifies your message and increases the customer's interest. It should be the easiest, clearest way to present the information in limited time and space. The right picture really is worth a thousand words, and so is the wrong picture! If the customer cannot understand the graphic in a few seconds, it's too complex.
- Keep your charts simple enough so that if the customer reviews them one week or one month later, they will remember your key messages on each one.
- Use an action verb to begin each bullet.
- Have a takeaway or "bumper sticker" on every chart. If you can't think of a meaningful takeaway for a chart, delete the entire chart.
- Be careful using animation and "build-ups." Used judiciously and appropriately, these are powerful techniques, but when overused they can quickly become very distracting.

Master's Tip: A Balanced Presentation Engages Every Member of Your Audience and Keeps Them Interested in What You Have to Say

Individuals interpret, grasp, and retain information very differently. Be respectful of this and realize that communication goes well beyond the words we choose or the charts we present. It's a fact that some people prefer text, some people prefer graphics, and some people prefer a balanced mix of the two. No two people receive and process information the same way. If your presentation is either too textual or too graphic, there's a high probability that you will alienate a part of your audience and lose their attention.

To avoid losing any member of your audience, try to include both text and graphics on every chart. If your presentation has a great deal of financial or numerical data, use both tables and complementing charts or graphs to show your information. Embedding a short video is also a very effective technique that you should use if it provides meaningful and pertinent information. Videos can also provide a refreshing break in your presentation that will be welcomed by everyone, including you.

Understand the audience's personality mix and perspective as best you can. Knowing this allows you to tune up your presentation to better suit and resonate with them.

When you are finished with a draft of your charts, ask several people with different backgrounds or skills to review your chart set for ease of understanding, accuracy, and consistency of numbers and facts throughout the entire presentation.

All charts must have a clear, easy-to-follow, and significant purpose. Throughout your preparation, continuously review your presentation to verify the following for each chart as well as for the end-to-end presentation:

- Is the format consistent and easy to read?
- Is every chart compliant and compatible with your customer's needs and requirements?
- Is the point of the chart and section clear?
- Do the charts, graphs, and pictures on a single chart complement and reinforce each other? Do they effectively communicate your message?
- Does the content reflect and reinforce your win strategy, value proposition, goals and objectives?
- Are you clearly showing features, benefits, discriminators, and key messages? Does each chart have a clean and meaningful takeaway (two lines max, concise summary, and lasting impression)?
- Does your artwork increase the customer's interest? Is it easy to understand?
- Is it customer-friendly? Will they understand and align with your purpose?

- Is it readable from the back of the presentation room and does it project well? Does it flow logically?
- Are the vital points clear and concise, or do you dull your point with too much data or text?
- Does an action verb begin each bullet?
- Is the data presented in the best format possible (e.g., pie chart versus line chart versus column versus tabular)?
- Are the numbers in the graphics clear? Do they effectively show comparisons, improvements, and solutions to previous problems?
- Is every chart and visual error free (one numerical or spelling mistake can start a snowball of distractions and skepticism)?
- Is there any self-contradictory information or inconsistency among all the charts?
- How can it be more effective?

Chapter 7 includes samples of winning charts that show the proper use and balance of illustrations, text, and use of color. They are included as examples to help you through the process of generating your presentation.

Master's Tip: Winners Know How to Make Complex Issues Seem Simple and Provide Solutions That Are Easy to Understand

No matter how complex a procurement is, there is always a way to summarize and capture your overall approach in a single graphic. This is not an easy task to accomplish, but generating this graphic can provide many benefits.

When your graphic is well executed, the customer will associate it uniquely with you! It will provide a memorable way for them to differentiate you from all of the other competitors.

Your charts must have enough content and information that they can "stand alone," and, following your presentation, become an excellent source of reference information for your customer.

Experience has shown that a well-done summary graphic is frequently used by customers in their decision-making process and may actually be used in the customer's internal decision-making briefings. This could occur immediately after you walk out the door, or it might be days, weeks, or months after your presentation. When a customer uses your chart to brief their management team, your probability of a win just got a whole lot better!

Some customers will compare information that is provided in your charts with information that is contained within your written proposal (if a written proposal is required, which it usually is). It is imperative that there are no disconnects or contradictions between these two documents. If you discover an inconsistency, it is your responsibility to bring this fact forward to the customer and to make crystal clear what is correct.

This is important contractually, both during the selection process and in the post-award environment. When contradictions do exist and are not brought to the customer's attention early in the process, it can lead to contractual issues at a later date. Or even worse, inconsistencies can help to substantiate a competitor's formal protest of an award that was made to you!

Effective Dialogue and Manuscript—The Key Part of Messaging Is Delivery

The *Mastering the Art of Oral Presentations* formula includes scripting for several reasons:

- Historically, the best speeches and presentations were the result of some form of scripting.
- Learning your script in advance results in a brilliant presentation, avoids the risk of rambling, and ensures you delete anything that doesn't create the desired impact or add value to your goals and objectives.

- Scripting ensures that your presentation conforms to time limitations while including the most important points (your approach, stories, win themes, and discriminators).
- If you know your script and timing well enough, you may be able to ad lib during the presentation to respond to nonverbal cues from the customer.
- Scripting, rehearsing, and learning the script creates confidence that can make the difference between success and failure.
- You will not have a chance to correct your content or messaging. Orals frequently represent your "best and final offer" to the customer, and sometimes may be your only opportunity to make a final proposal revision before the customer makes a buying decision. Therefore, orals are your last opportunity to influence the customer in your favor. Errors at this stage of the procurement can be fatal.

Preparation and presenting based on a script is not easy. The first step is to write the most effective script. The second is to rehearse the script until it becomes second nature to you.

Your script should evolve from your presentation outline, your win strategy, and by default, your customer's requirements and hot buttons. As you develop your script, for timing purposes, plan on a delivery speed of about 125 words per minute (wpm). In a relaxed, everyday conversational environment, most people talk at a rate of 120 to 140 wpm. Using 125 wpm for planning purposes seems to work out about right for most people making formal oral presentations.

Your orals coach will help you fine tune your presentation, so don't get hung up on absolute numbers. Initially, simply get the important information down on paper and into your script; you can add or subtract content later.

To memorize your script will take you between 20 and 30 repetitions. To start, practice out loud on your own in private. Reading the script to yourself in silence won't get you where you need to be: do it out loud. Stand up, project with your vocal presentation volume, and use natural arm gestures and body movement. This may seem silly, but experience shows that it really works.

After you gain some confidence, start reciting your script in front of a few people or in private with your orals coach. Allow plenty of time to do this. Keep doing this until you have committed your script to memory and are comfortable with it.

So here's the trick. The goal of using and memorizing a script is not to deliver it verbatim to your audience. The goal is to learn what you are going to say so that you can deliver your message to your audience in a natural way. The memorization of a script allows you to be totally comfortable with the content and to ensure that you do not miss any of the key messages. Memorizing your script will also enable you to be much more relaxed during the formal presentation.

A side benefit of a great script is that it's a lifesaver to your backup if for some reason you're not able to attend the formal presentation. There are numerous unforeseeable reasons you may not be able to attend, and if you cannot, your backup will rely heavily on your script to ensure the right message is delivered. Your backup and your entire team will thank you profusely for a well prepared and well rehearsed script.

So, in a nutshell, take the time needed to prepare a perfect script, commit your script to memory, rehearse it until you've perfected its delivery, share it with your backup, and capitalize on the fruits of your labor at the formal presentation!

Introductions

Typically, the lead customer will introduce the customer's evaluation team and invite your team to introduce your participants before beginning the formal (and frequently timed) portion of the presentation. The highest ranking member of your presentation team should provide this introduction, briefly stating: (1) each person's name; (2) each person's current position; (3) Why each was selected; (4) each person's proposed position and qualifications for the position; (5) How each relates to the requirements and how each will benefit the customer.

You should know this information for every other member of your team in case you are asked about it during a Q&A session. A good introduction enables the first speaker to begin the presentation with meaningful content.

Good terms to use in describing personnel during team introductions include the following:

- Experienced
- Reliable
- Innovative
- Supportive

- Responsive
- Qualified
- Creative

During the presentation, assume that the customer will forget names and titles for everyone except your first speaker (typically the highest ranking member of the presentation team), and it will be necessary for each presenter to introduce the next. This introduction must be short, relevant, and enable the next presenter to begin with an opening statement. To save time, this can occur while the presenter approaches the front of the room. Without compromising your time constraints, consider including the following when you introduce the next presenter:

- The presenter's name and role on the contract and/or the proposal.
- The presenter's relevant background and experience.
- Why customers will be interested in the presenter's section.

You must convey that you have a close working relationship with the presenter you introduce.

Sample introductions:

- It is my pleasure to introduce my colleague, John Doe, an experienced (contract job title) with more than XX years serving this customer community as (relevant job title). John's approach to (topic) has successfully reduced cost and risk in [similar environment(s)], and he has a solid approach to achieving the same results for you.

- My long-time co-worker and friend, Mary Smith, brings XX years of directly relevant experience to her proposed position of (contract job title). She will share her lessons learned and how they have continued to influence her (work process/approach) to provide XX% improvement in (something) year-over-year.
- Dr. Elizabeth Jones is renowned in the (identified) field, and we are proud to have her as our proposed (contract position). Her (amazing, industry-acknowledged accomplishments) are directly applicable to some of the challenges you are facing, and she has an innovative approach to implementing (something related) for you.
- With over XX years of experience, Don Schmidt, our onsite manager of human resources, has demonstrated his ability to enhance labor relations and improve employee morale at (contract site).
- Mr. Charles Brown is our proposed business office manager. Charlie brings unique business management talent that comes from over XX years of experience in aerospace business systems supporting both government and commercial customers.

Getting Started

Your presentation should have a common look and feel that extends beyond the common format of your graphics and visuals. The additional common element is how you present your material.

Presenters should follow a common pattern and common ground rules:

- Avoid any reference to politics, current or previous administrations, or names of leaders or companies, because this may cause customers to react emotionally. Emotional responses, whether negative or positive, should be avoided unless you are absolutely sure the response will be positive.
- Weave into every part of your message: (1) operational excellence; (2) best practices; (3) ownership; (4) communication, (5) commitment; (6) value.

- Avoid posh language and big words that you wouldn't normally use, because it will make you appear arrogant.
- Keep it simple and do it well. Develop confidence in your ability to present your material. Avoid anything that makes your presentation appear too complicated or defensive.
- By all means, avoid arrogance.

As you begin to develop your script, hang a copy of your charts on a wall in the correct order. With a red marker, work with your orals coach to identify and label each chart's priority as H (high), M (medium), or L (low) to help determine how much time you'll spend on each. Tape a blank piece of paper below each chart. On the blank sheet write the two or three key messages for that chart. This will help you prepare and refine your script.

As shown in Figure 3.1, the first minute of your presentation and the last 30 seconds are the two most important parts. Far more time

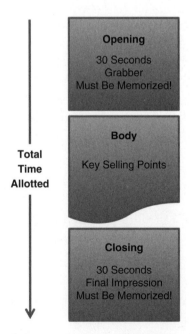

Figure 3.1 Planning your presentation timeline

and attention should be devoted to preparing these sections than anything else. The first minute must include an opening statement to get the customer's attention and make them want to pay attention to the rest of your presentation. It is your "grabber" and can be thought of as the "teaser." Remember, the audience spends about the first three minutes of the presentation sizing up the presenter. Use this time to open with impact and make an impression that will endure throughout your entire presentation.

The last 30 seconds is the closing statement that leaves the final impression. The all-important sell is in the body.

Preparing Opening and Closing Statements

The opening statement should directly reference, or provide an answer to, the customer's needs and requirements, and should:

- Get the customer's attention.
- Make them want to hear the rest of your section.
- Follow smoothly from the previous section.
- Hint at the sell portion of your section.

Which of the following two opening statements is more effective?

- The speaker stands and says, "My part consists of telling you about our manufacturing capability. We follow three phases of production…"
  or

- The speaker stands, holds up a piece of equipment and says, "We will decrease your operating cost by 20% and increase reliability by over 65%. We will do this by implementing this technology and others in a remarkable way…"

As you develop your opening statement, consider the following approaches:

- Ask a challenging and intriguing question that you know the customer will identify with.
- Present a short scenario to which the customer can relate.
- Address one of the customer's hot buttons.

Here are a few sample opening statements using NASA as the customer:

- 23 years ago I chose to support NASA, and I've never regretted that decision. Why? Because of the mission, the people, and the challenging work that NASA does. The human space flight community is unique and amazing. I have the deepest respect for the importance of the mission, the talents of the people who support it, and the criticality of the systems that take humans into space.
- I'm very happy to be here today, and am proud to be the human resources manager for (contractor) here at the (customer site). My job is all about people, and ultimately, people are what make any business or bold new endeavor a success.
- We didn't get it completely right the first time. But, we kept learning from our mistakes and improving our algorithms and models. We can now offer you an optimized approach to simulation that's currently saving several of our customers more than XX% on each instrument they develop.
  - (Note that this opening statement admits that there have been failures in the past. However, it also shows that lessons have been learned and corrective measures have been taken. The customer now benefits from valuable lessons learned and respects your honesty. Be careful how you present this type of information and ensure there is a positive, beneficial outcome.)
- My passion for propulsion testing began with my first assignment here at (customer site). Conducting a rocket main engine firing test is one of the most exciting things I've ever done. Today, I'm just as excited each time my team conducts a firing. Just when I thought the experience couldn't be beaten, I was asked to join (Astronaut Name) here in the rotunda to receive the Silver Snoopy

award [Note: this is a prestigious, real-world NASA award] for conducting over a million thruster firings. New opportunities led me to management roles at other test centers but when I got the chance to return to (customer site), I jumped at it! As my career has changed from engineering to management, so have the challenges that excite me. Managing, mentoring, and leading the propulsion department is as exciting to me today as those early main engine firings were!

The closing statement is equally important. It must create a strong, lasting impression. Ideally, your closing statement will undeniably state the unique value your team offers the customer in your presentation section. It is the one statement you want the customer to remember even if they forget everything else you say.

When generating your closing statement, consider the following:

- Does it summarize the benefit of your team's approach in this section?
- Does it follow smoothly from the body of your section?
- Does it flow smoothly to the next presenter's section?
- Is it succinct and impactful? Will they remember it in a week?
- Does it leave the customer feeling as though they want to work with you more than with any other team?

Your closing is the last point that the customer will hear from you. It must be as strong as your opening—well rehearsed and compelling. The customer will remember your opening and closing statements more than any other part of your presentation. And they'll always remember how you made them feel.

Sample closing statements:

- Finally, in summary, our approach will ensure mission success while reducing operational cost by XX%. We've demonstrated that our approach is very reliable and exceeds mission requirements. This margin of safety ensures mission success ... your success ... to which we are fully and deeply committed.

- Together we can capitalize on our demonstrated, solid, and productive performance to further expand the (customer's/facility) capabilities and ensure a strong and exciting future for (customer/mission).
- Our team has demonstrated that we have the vision and insight needed to blend (customer) unique talent, new ideas and capabilities, and corporate and technical skills from both (prime contractor) and our teammates to achieve (customer) mission success. We will do the same for you!
- We are proud of what we've helped the site accomplish during our tenure here, and we're excited about, and profoundly committed to, our role in its future.
- We fully understand and have demonstrated our ability to accomplish the work by exceeding your requirements and expectations while reducing cost.
- As your information technology provider, our ultimate goal is to be ridiculously reliable and user-transparent, so when the users arrive at their desks in the morning and turn on their computers and tools … they just work. We have proven time and again that we can do this for other customers, now we want to do it for you!

Preparing the Body of Your Presentation

The body of your section of the presentation is the "sell" portion. Each chart serves the dual purpose of addressing the customer's formal and informal buying criteria and convincing them that your solution is the best. As you begin developing your script, start with the notes you posted on the wall beneath each of your charts and write out a more detailed explanation. This is the beginning of creating your story and is the basis for your script. Look for the discriminators in your section, and practice how you will emphasize them vocally.

As with the opening and closing of your section, the opening and closing statements for each chart are the most important and present the messages that the customer is most likely to remember. They must initially grab the customer's attention and undeniably demonstrate how your team adds value.

- To help you script your briefing, apply the following winning, yet simple formula to each point you make:
  - State the "what"—clearly and simply.
  - State the "how"—clearly and objectively.
  - State one or two key strengths or discriminators offered by your team and clarify why these are important—give two or three concise examples of these.
  - State how this will benefit the customer (answer the "so what?").
  - End with a strong summary statement—your takeaway or tag line.
- Keep everything positive and avoid any negatives.
- Use short sentences and short paragraphs.
- Clearly define your acronyms, jargon, and familiar terms the first time you use them.
- Memorize every opening and takeaway!
- Practice your portion of the presentation until you can present each of your charts with only brief, occasional glances at your script. This enables you to spend 90% of your time squarely looking at the audience.

When you know your content and your script, you can concentrate on delivery. Delivery is the only way your message is received, and it's your job to deliver your message in such a way that the customer perceives your team as the most desirable supplier.

Refining Your Message—Improvements to Increase Your Win Probability

After you have a baseline of your charts and script, and as you begin practicing, either individually or with other presenters, you will also begin refining your messaging to improve the quality and content of your presentation. Refinements will better reinforce or reflect other presenters' material, strengthen your intended messaging, include value-added material from the team's prework, and/or improve the flow of the end-to-end presentation.

There are key messages that every team needs to convey to the customer. These include both direct messages shown in the content of your script and charts, and indirect messages that are conveyed by each presenter's demeanor and attitude during the presentation.

Any member of the team can convey direct messages, however, all members of the team must convey indirect messages. Consider the messaging in Table 3.2 as you refine and practice your material. Pay specific attention to how you convey both direct and indirect messages.

In addition to this messaging, consider the following refinements to improve your presentation material:

- Define and quantify any and all metrics that will guide and drive improvement across the program.
- Make sure all timelines and schedules are compliant and clear; build in and address prudent time reserves to minimize implementation risk.
- Stress the advantages, benefits, and features of working with your team.
- Explain any ambiguous terms.
- Make sure you have enough evidence to illustrate and support your case.
- Your evidence must be objective, and must clearly illustrate, validate, convince, and inspire.
- Present your solution and support it with examples; repeat this process over and over.
- Be absolutely certain your content covers every major customer requirement and hot button.
- Every chart must show something unique about your team and its offering.
  - The primary recurring theme is "benefits to the customer."
  - Show how each thought, idea or action will be beneficial to the customer.
- Your entire presentation should tell a story.
  - This is an art form that goes far beyond just being compliant with the requirements.
  - Spend considerable time working together as a team as you begin to develop and refine your messaging.

- It is essential that you carefully decide what your story is and how to tell it.
- When your senior executives visit your team during your preparation process, you should be able to easily and simply tell them your story.

As you prepare and refine your presentation, continuously review it to ensure:

- You are supporting your win strategy.
- You reinforce your value proposition.
- All of your win themes and discriminators are included and reinforced.
- You address all of the customer's hot buttons.
- Each major chart has a thoughtful and meaningful takeaway.

Table 3.2   Examples of Direct and Indirect Messages

Content—Sample Direct Messages	Delivery—Essential Indirect Messages
Ongoing communication	Responsiveness
Superior access to best practices	Credibility
Quality	Trust
Discriminators	Experience, capability, competence
Benefits	Judgment
Technical requirements	Competence
Risk mitigation	Commitment
Experience / Past performance	Success
Reporting: formal, informal, in-person, other	Relationships – among team and customer
Processes and their maturity	Integrity
Geographic presence	Depth of team knowledge and experience
Value-added solutions	Value-added leadership
Fresh perspective	Creativity
Innovation	Transformation
Qualified subcontractors/vendors	Confidence
Breadth and depth of team	Professionalism and resources

Review the Power of Your Language—What You Say and How You Say It Are Equally Important

Specifically selected language can be used to shift an audience from purely passive listeners to active listeners. Some techniques to encourage active listening include:

Emphasize	"A particularly important factor…"
Repeat	"Twenty-two events a day. Twenty-two!"
Restate	"Let's look at that another way."
Bridge	"We've seen the causes and effects: Let's examine possible solutions."
Question	"So what is the best choice?"
Invite	"Put yourselves in their position."
Enumerate	"The first point is…"

Do not overuse any of these techniques. As you apply them be very selective with both when and how they are used.

An optimal approach is to use them to focus on your discriminators, the value proposition, and the customer's hot buttons. When properly used in this context, the most important aspects of your presentation will become even more memorable.

As you generate, review, and practice your presentation, attend to the specific language you use and make sure you address the following:

- Beware of language that may be even slightly interpreted as offensive with respect to ethnicity, religion, politics, gender, age, socioeconomic status, and cultural background.
- Always be truthful!
- Avoid sarcasm, criticism, self-deprecation, arrogance, cynicism, or defensive language.
- Train yourself to use an active voice rather than a passive voice as you construct your presentation. Active voice creates stronger, more compelling imagery than passive voice.

- An example of passive voice: "The performance of the team was brilliant."
- An active voice would say: "The team brilliantly surpassed previous performance records."

Make Your Content Work for You—Achieve the Most Value with Limited Time and Resources

Since your presentation time is limited, make sure the content you select is relevant, meaningful, and delivers your key messages and discriminators. Stories are far more memorable than statistics.

Apply the following tips:

- Present from the perspective that you must earn the customer's attention.
- Analogies can be very powerful, but don't use them to excess.
- Citing sources that are known and respected by the customer will greatly enhance your indirect messaging.
- Do not underestimate the power of personal stories that have given you your experience and knowledge, and consequently, the right to be part of the team. Feel confident using some of these personal experiences to illustrate points in your presentation.
- Select your evidence very carefully. Your goal is to clarify, elaborate, and support your claims while exciting your audience.
- Use specific details as opposed to general statements.
- Highlight pertinent and impressive numbers, quantities, schedule or technical breakthroughs, and cost reductions.
- Use anything that will grab the audience and highlight your team's successful past performance.

Your presentation is really like a formal job interview, and to some degree, a stage show.

Highlighting Strengths and Mitigating Weaknesses—All Companies Have Them, so Know Yours!

Every company has strengths and weaknesses. Prepare content that will highlight the former and mitigate the latter.

Master's Tip: Always Address Risk Directly and Objectively

When it comes to dealing with risk, there is no substitute for experience. If you have good applicable experience, tell how you have managed similar risks in the past and tell how this procurement benefits from your experiences.

One of the few advantages an incumbent has is that of understanding relevant risks and knowing how to manage them. This is a tremendous advantage over less experienced competitors. Not knowing a risk and understanding how to successfully deal with it, such as those that a less experienced competitor may not know, can be a disaster. If you are less experienced and fighting a strong competitor, take time to think through all the risks you may experience during the course of the contract.

Bring in people to help you who are domain experts and discuss risks with them. Get lots of opinions relative to risk identification and how to mitigate every one of them.

One word of caution: be sure that the risks you bring forward are real. Don't fabricate or exaggerate a risk just for the sake of having something to talk about!

The following will help you successfully accomplish this goal:

- Continually reinforce your claim of "We are your choice!" with "Here's why!" Do not make the customer search for a reason to choose you.
- Although you should honestly acknowledge any potential risks associated with your proposal, you must also mitigate the effect of

acknowledging the risk. If you have a "risk" chart, ensure that every risk is fully explained and fully mitigated. Never trivialize risks. Doing so could make the difference between winning and losing. Take real and perceived risks very seriously and never downplay them.

- Change negatives to positives. Refer to past errors, issues, and mistakes as opportunities to improve and show that you have learned from the past. Doing this can become a competitive advantage. Emphasize how these situations have given you the opportunity to implement successful solutions, develop the ability to adapt, and improve resilience.
- Be able to answer:
  - "Why are we successful?"
  - "What are we really good at?"
  - "Why are we the best?"
  - "Why are we your choice?"
  - "Why are we qualified to do this work?"
- Be able to explain:
  - "Why was I selected to be on this team?"
  - "Why and how will I bring value to you?"
- Key messages to weave throughout the presentation:
  - "We understand your values and have structured our approach to fully support and enforce them."
  - "We have designed our solution to focus on your priorities."
  - "Your objectives are our objectives."
- Demonstrate that you enjoy, trust, and depend on each other as a team; that you know, understand, and leverage each other's strengths.
- Give examples of why you are "low risk." For example:
  - Low risk in program transition. If you're the incumbent, "We are already in place. You know us."
  - Low risk due to minimal learning curve.
  - Low risk because our performance metrics demonstrate and fully support this!
  - Low risk due to our proven technical and management solution.

- Remember that your real purpose is to help the customer make a decision in your favor and award the contract to you.
- Emphasize innovation.
- Repeatedly highlight your discriminators.
- If you are absolutely, unconditionally, and unquestionably certain of your facts, address very carefully and discreetly any "negatives" that the incumbent has with the customer by showing what you will do differently. Do not use competing company names or names of individuals. Attack the issue, not the individuals or company.
- Anticipate and address questions the customer is likely to have.

Master's Tip: Use Trade Studies to Strengthen Your Position and Weaken That of Your Competitors

A strong incumbent will be acutely aware of its weaknesses and will have done everything possible to mitigate them, including making a complete change in its approach. Ghosting the competition can be very effective but it can backfire on you if you ghost a nonexistent issue!

A more effective and less risky approach to discrediting the competition is to perform objective trade studies on alternate approaches. Within your trade space, include what you believe to be the approach of the current incumbent contractor and likely competitors. Doing this shows you truly understand all the issues and have taken the time to thoughtfully work through them. This shows you have optimized your approach by using clear thinking and keeping the customer's needs and requirements in total focus. Trade studies are also a great help to customers who may not have the time, resources, or talent to perform the trades themselves. Do your trades and do them well; you will never regret it!

Using Content and Delivery to Connect

If You Don't Connect, You're Just Another Presenter

There are several useful phrases and considerations that will help you connect with your audience and answer the nagging question, "What's in it for me?" For example:

- "…which we recognize is very important to you."
- "…which we know is one of your key objectives."
- "Let me illustrate this with something we know is important to you…"
- "You will experience a major improvement in…or satisfy your major objective of…when we…"
- "…which will make your life easier by…"
- "…which, from your perspective, will…"
- "The reason why this is critical to you is…"
- "This is how you'll experience significant savings…"
- "How does this benefit you? The answer is…"
- "You might ask, "Why?" Well,…"
- "Here's why we feel this is essential to your needs…"
- "We believe this is vital to your customer because…"

Double check your content by asking yourself, your team, and your reviewers: "Will any of our charts or statements bring up any negative associations in the minds of the customer?"

Anticipate the customer's questions and answer them in the body of the presentation. This will reduce the Q&A time and increase their trust in your competence.

Consider the following techniques to help improve your win probability:

- Use numbers, facts, percentages, and statistics rather than vague "aren't we wonderful" adjectives that anyone could say.
- Always put yourself in the shoes of the customer; be empathetic. Look at everything you say and claim you will do from their perspective. Remember they are always asking, "What's in it for me?"

- Make sure every claim is solid and fully supported. Never make unsubstantiated or puffed-up claims. The customer will most likely fact-check and verify your claims.
- Don't ever assume the customer knows your strengths; tell them what they are. Conversely, you should assume they know your weaknesses; compensate for them.
- Everything you say must reinforce in their minds that you clearly understand their requirements.
- Conveying arrogance almost ensures you will lose. Your challenge is to achieve a balance between confidence, competence, and humility.
- Use the word *you* frequently to personalize your message to your audience.
- The audience, especially if it is more than one or two people, does have human limits to their understanding and ability to grasp a variety of complex issues. None of us are experts in everything! Keep your presentation as simple and clear as possible.
- Whenever you give an example from your past, take advantage of a "connecting opportunity" by saying "and we can do this for you ..."
- Try to include these phrases:
  - "We understand your requirements because of our experiences with ..."
  - "We recognize and appreciate your concerns ..."
  - "We can relate to your internal customer's expectations ..."

Incumbent Tips

Never Assume It's Yours to Lose ... or You Will Indeed Lose!

If you are the incumbent, emphasize the benefit of any and all past performance (both positive and negative). Consider including these statements:

- Here is how we solved your challenges in the past (if you have positive experience).
- Here is how we currently solve your challenges (if you have positive experience).

- Here is how we will solve your future challenges.
- Here is what we have learned from past challenges and what we are doing to prevent negative experiences from ever happening again.

> **Master's Tip: Capitalize on Past Successes and Turn Weaknesses into Strengths**
>
> Capitalize on past performance successes, but do not sidestep any issues or problems you may have had in the past. Always be truthful and don't exaggerate or deflate any facts. Acknowledge whatever issues you did have and tell how they were overcome. Show that you have learned from prior problems and that you are now even stronger since you have successfully dealt with them. Knowing where real challenges exist and having a plan to manage them successfully also reduces risk. This is a real plus for any incumbent. In short, if there have been problems in the past, address them directly and make them work to your advantage. Don't try to mask them or simply omit them from your presentation. Doing so will erode your credibility. Be honest and straightforward. Show that you understand where you went wrong in the past and turn any weakness into a strength.

Leverage all the benefits of being the incumbent. For example:

- Find ways to quantify and place a value on the transition cost from the current contract to the new one.
  - Compute the actual value of your savings (an absolute value or a percentage) through a rigorous financial and engineering analysis.
  - Factor in the cost of having two contractors working during a transition phase.
  - Remind the customer of the cost of educating a new contractor on the processes, procedures, sensitivities, and nuances of the customer organization.

- Cite examples of how changing to a new contractor has adversely affected the productivity and morale of the workforce. Quantify this using historical metrics such as learning curves associated with productivity, safety records, and so on.
- If an existing approach is to be used, don't suffer the complacency of "incumbentitis." Be prepared to tell why you selected that approach, and the answer cannot be, "Because we have always done it that way." A new approach always requires explanation and justification, and so does an existing one!
- How would you improve what you do today? New approaches and methods may work better and be more cost effective.
- Look for changes that may be quicker and less expensive. Cost is always a driver.
- Use brief, well-known examples only when they will support and give credibility to the selected approaches and methods in a chart. If the customer participated in the approach, and it worked, you achieve instant credibility.
- Emphasize things you have done and learned on the current contract that the competition cannot claim.
- Demonstrate the lower risks to the customer: they already know you; nominal or zero learning curve; technical/management solutions and performance metrics already proven within their organization.
- Pretend you are not the incumbent when you are designing your solution. What would you do better to beat the incumbent?

You are generating a marketing document designed to sell the desired capability to the customer. Direct, succinct facts and approaches are the key to telling the customer how you plan to accomplish the tasks in the new contract.

Master's Tip: Use an Independent Team to Design a "Clean-Sheet" Solution

If you are the incumbent, consider pulling together a truly independent team of experts to design an approach via a "clean sheet of paper" using only the procurement requirements document as a starting point. Don't try to influence them in any way and keep them away from people who might try to sway their decision-making. Take the inputs from the independent team and study them carefully. Modify your approach where you see benefits. Never assume that you know better because you "know what the customer really wants."

Chapter 4

Rehearse

The Delivery — Part Interview, Part Stage Show

T he success of your presentation is directly proportional to the investment you make in preparation time. You never get a second chance to make a good first impression, no matter how well you know the customer or the members of the selection committee.

Remember, they have not seen you in this role for this contract. A new contract means a new you!

With the very first chart and the preliminary introductions, the customer is evaluating you in this context and deciding if you understand their needs and requirements. They are also developing their answers to the all-important questions, "What's in it for me?" and "Do I want to work with them?"

You have spent time selecting, developing, and refining your presentation content, both charts and script. Now the real work begins: ensuring you are optimally prepared for your final presentation to the customer.

As shown in Figure 4.1, and according to the Association of Proposal Management Professionals, visual image creates approximately 55% of the presentation's impact (appearance of presenters and charts), vocals create 38% of the impact (the sound of the presenters' voices), and content is responsible for only the final 7%.

The impact of your personal visuals and voice is derived partially from preparation but primarily from practice. This includes the confidence and competence you project.

You have four powerful personal tools at your disposal when delivering your presentation:

- Vocal and verbal: your *story* and your *voice.*
- Nonverbal: your *face* (especially your smile and your eyes) and your *appearance*, including body language.

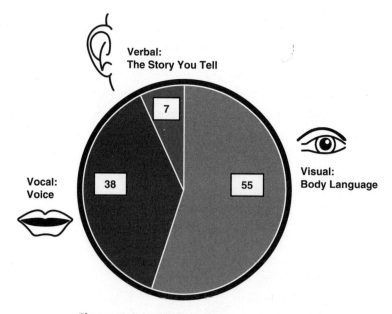

Figure 4.1   Elements of Presentation Impact

Appearance

Appearance Is a Major Factor—Use It to Your Advantage

Your appearance should reflect respect for the customer. Just as for a job interview, your dress must be professional, conservative, classic, clean, and your clothing must fit well. In addition, follow the "seven-points" rule. A "point" is anything beyond your clothing that could distract the evaluators. Points include earrings, necklaces, bracelets, rings, watches, glasses, belts (especially buckles), hair ornaments, nail polish, ties, tie tacks, cufflinks, and vests. You should have seven or fewer "points."

For example, a presenter's seven points may be a wedding ring, glasses, a watch, nail polish, a necklace, a pair of earrings, and a bracelet. A person with double ear piercings who wears two pairs of earrings should count these as two points.

As a general rule of thumb, inappropriate or ill-fitting clothing will be distracting to the audience. It could cause customers to unfairly judge or label you as incompetent, sloppy, unprofessional, poorly prepared, uncommitted, or insecure; not the image they want to represent them in their business world.

Appropriate attire conveys your sense of professionalism and the importance of the event. Consider the following general rules and guide-lines when selecting your presentation attire. Align your dress with that of your customers. Don't make them feel uncomfortable by overdressing, but don't underdress either. Understand your customer's environment and culture and dress to show respect that is commensurate with the event.

- Wear dark blue, gray, charcoal, or black.
- No brown suits or dresses.
- Wear a white or light blue shirt or blouse.
- Wear a power tie (predominantly blue or burgundy, small print).
- The tie should just touch the top of the belt buckle.
- No bow ties, double-breasted suits, or cufflinks.
- Keep a clean handkerchief concealed in your pocket. This can be used to dab sweat from your chin, nose, or forehead, in extreme cases.

- Undergarments must be covered and out of sight.
- No cleavage.
- No short skirts above the knee. Note how the skirt fits and appears when you are seated.
- Your clothing should not be wrinkled, ripped, soiled, missing buttons, or out of style.
- Shoes must be polished, and should be properly soled and heeled; they should not appear worn out.
- No open/peep toe shoes or sandals.
- Hosiery must be free of runs or snags.
- Men's pants cuffs should not be above the top of socks when seated.
- Coat and jacket lining should not hang below the hem.
- No item of clothing should appear too big or too small.
- Realistically, many of us are now carrying a few extra pounds. We, therefore, must be sure that our choice of clothing fits us adequately. It should drape the body and not be tight anywhere.
  - Make sure that blouses and shirts are not pulling at the buttons.
  - Make sure there is ample room at the stomach and in the seat of your clothing.
- Use a full length, preferably three-way mirror (to see yourself from all angles) when you select your attire.

In addition to your clothing, consider the following recommendations regarding hair, grooming, and accessories:

- Never try a new haircut, hairstyle, or color just prior to your presentation (if you do, you may be overly self-conscious, which will distract you from your focus).
- If you need, or will need, a haircut, get it at least four or five days prior to the presentation.
- Make sure your hairstyle does not cover your eyebrows or eyes—this blocks your facial expressions.
- Dandruff and bad breath in close quarters can be very distracting. Get help if needed.

- Avoid using overly perfumed products. Some people are allergic to fragrances.
- If you have a beard or mustache, make sure it is trimmed and away from your lips, so as not to distract the customer or interfere with your diction.
- Eyebrows should be well groomed and check for stray hairs in and on your nose/chin.
- Nails should be well groomed and, if possible, professionally done; they should be conservative in color, length, and design.
- Makeup and lipstick should be understated, not dramatic or garish, to enhance the appearance and not distract the audience.
- Avoid jewelry that is overly large or ornate. Like your attire, jewelry should be conservative. If you are prone to nervousness, beware of the tendency to play with your rings, which can be distracting.
- Avoid charm bracelets and anything that rattles, clinks, or jingles (including pocket change).
- There should be no visible body piercings except for ears.
- There should be no visible tattoos.
- Don't have anything in your pockets or around you that you could twist, shred, bend, or unravel (toothpick, paper clip, twist tie, tissue, straw, coffee stirrer). From the customer's vantage point, it will make you look very insecure and not in control.
- If you are a smoker, take steps to prevent your hair, clothes, breath, and things from smelling of smoke.

Prepare for a clothing inspection approximately one week prior to orals.

Verbal Delivery Tips

Learn, Practice and Use Words to Create Impact
Verbal delivery includes your rate, volume, pitch, and pauses. Each aspect is critical to conveying your message effectively. If your audience doesn't understand your words, they will not understand your message. Use your voice to animate, energize, focus, emphasize, engage, and connect with the audience.

Rate is the speed at which you speak. Because the customer has intimate knowledge of the topic and requirements, their rate of cognitive comprehension will be roughly 8 to 10 times faster than the average presenter speaks. Consequently, your challenge is to keep the customer's mind from straying or wandering.

Deliberately select a rate of speed that corresponds to the message or topic being presented. For example, when briefing a busy chart, it is appropriate to slow your rate to guide the audience through the chart. When briefing charts that are more self-explanatory, a faster rate may be appropriate. Select the speed that is best suited to guiding the customer's thinking. Vary the speed to help maintain interest.

Volume is the loudness or softness of your voice. As with speed, deliberately select the appropriate volume for each point or message, and vary volume to create and maintain interest.

Speaking quietly requires the audience to pay careful attention and can be an attention grabber. Louder volume can also be used to stress specific points, but beware that you are not perceived as shouting at the audience. Louder volume, beyond adequately projecting so you can be heard, should be used sparingly.

Pitch is how high or low your voice is. Changes in pitch are synonymous with vocal inflections. When you use a monotone, it conveys that you have nothing terribly interesting to present. When you vary your pitch, it helps emphasize important points, including leading questions. As with speed and volume, deliberately vary your pitch.

Pauses add color and expression when used effectively. You may pause before introducing a new idea, or after making a point to add impact. Pauses must be silent; "um, er, or uh" will delete the impact and may even be annoying or distracting to the audience.

Inflection and emphasis can completely alter the message even when the words are identical. For example: read the following sentence six times, each time emphasizing the italicized word, and see how the meaning changes.

- "*He* did not say she lied about the error." Then WHO really did say it?
- "He did *not* say she lied about the error." Then WHAT was actually said?
- "He did not *say* she lied about the error." Then HOW was it actually communicated?
- "He did not say *she* lied about the error." Then WHO did lie?
- "He did not say she *lied* about the error." Then WHAT did she actually do?
- "He did not say she lied about the *error.*" Then WHAT did she lie about?

Fairly, or unfairly, people judge us by our language, so it is important to use correct vocabulary and grammar, and avoid the following common errors:

- **Irregardless**–not a word; in its place, use regardless or irrespective.
- **Orientate**–not a word; use orient or familiarize.
- **Very unique**–there are no degrees to uniqueness. It is like dead–you either are or you aren't. Use unique (but if you do use this word, be absolutely certain that whatever it is meets the definition of unique).
- **Administrate**–not a word; use administer.
- **Continuous versus continual**–they are not synonymous. Continuous means something happens without stopping. Continual means something happens frequently. Use them correctly.
- **Hopefully**–frequently used incorrectly. Wrong: "Hopefully, we will be able to provide low cost…" Correct: "We looked hopefully to the future." Hopefully is an adverb. Try not to use hopefully at all; it conveys uncertainty!
- **Less versus fewer**–they are not synonymous. Fewer is used with things that can be counted. Less refers to mass or space—for example, "There is less waste if we have fewer mistakes on the line."
- **Anxious versus eager**–they are not synonymous. Anxious means filled with anxiety or worry. Eager means enthusiastic about

doing something. Incorrect: "We are anxious to get started." Correct: "We are eager to get started."

Your vocabulary and grammar can enhance or detract from your vocal delivery, and it will result in predictable benefits or consequences. Your orals or speech coach will help you avoid the misuse of words.

> **Master's Tip: Always Be Positive, Upbeat, and Confident!**
>
> Always be positive! Customers don't want to hear about problems, they want to hear about answers and great solutions. They don't want to hear about unbounded risks, they want to hear about risk eliminators, or at the very least, risk mitigators. They don't want to hear about unknown costs, they want to hear about bounded and well-understood costs. They don't want to hear how tough the design requirements are, they want to hear about innovative approaches and designs that improve performance.
>
> Whenever you see something that comes across in your presentation as a negative, turn it into a positive.

In addition to your rate, volume, pitch, and pauses, apply the following verbal delivery tips:

- Scripts must not be read. To learn each part, first use your full script, then reduce that to notes, then reduce that to one small card with key word triggers, then use nothing. The charts gradually become the triggers.
- Converse with the customer. Don't read to them.
- Never talk down to the audience.
- Convey conviction. Believe in what you are saying. Make sure your conviction is obvious to the audience.

- Don't trail off. Keep your voice strong, so there is no doubt that they can hear the last two or three words of each sentence.
- Use vocal variety for emphasis.
- Avoid "vocal static." Vocal static is the general term to refer to audible fillers that are the result of nervousness and uncertainty. They include "um, uh, uh-huh, er, okay, you know, well, so," and others.
- E-NUN-CI-ATE!
- No gum, mints, or candy!
- Do not end sentences with "okay?" or "ya."
- Do not end sentences by using an increased pitch emphasis on the last word (making the sentence sound like a question).
- Avoid trite or trendy phrases and clichés. Be original and clever in developing new ways of saying old things.
- Don't talk too quickly, or too slowly.
- Avoid terms of uncertainty (would, could, should, think, hope, believe, might) and replace them with positive and certain terms (will, know, understand, etc.).
- Reinforce your "takeaways" or "bumper stickers" on your charts.
- Use inflection to emphasize your discriminators.
- Change your cadence or rhythm at the end of each chart to emphasize your final statement.
- Be assertively positive in your phrases and terms as noted in Table 4.1.
- The last statement the customer hears must convey that, "We look forward to working with you."

Table 4.1 Weak versus Assertive Phrases

Weak	Assertive
"I think you will see…"	"You will see…"
"We believe you will find…"	"You will find…"
"We should be able to…"	"We will be able to…"
"We feel we are an ideal team member…"	"We are an ideal member…"

As you rehearse, remember that natural conversational tones and appearance are the most pleasant for the audience. Practice until you have mastered the application of these tools and techniques. Dress for success but retain your natural style and be comfortable. Be polished, positive, and professional while doing what you do better than anyone in the universe—being you—which is why you were chosen as a presenter!

Nonverbal Delivery Tips

Your Actions Speak More Loudly Than Your Words

Although verbal delivery (tone, pitch, volume, pauses) contributes to approximately 38% of presentation effectiveness, researchers have confirmed that about 55% is derived from nonverbal communication, including facial expressions and body language. Since how you look and act conveys more meaning and influence to the audience than what you say, you need to make sure your verbal and nonverbal communication reinforce the same message.

As you rehearse, keep these facts in mind:

- Hand gestures can add value or can be a source of distraction.
- Facial expressions are critical: they consciously and subconsciously convey messages (anger, fear, boredom, excitement, doubt, surprise, pleasure, pain).
- Good posture improves your ability to project your voice while reflecting professionalism and competence.

The audience will be especially focused on your personal demeanor during the first five minutes of your presentation. As you proceed, any and all actions will provide continuous nonverbal communication. You should appear natural, relaxed, confident, and reasonable from the time you stand up to approach the podium until you return to your seat.

Your nonverbal mannerisms and messages can send desirable or undesirable signals in the eyes of the customer.

- Positive and desirable nonverbal messages include:
  - Mature, professional, credible, capable, skilled, strong, confident, together, competent, in control, authentic, approachable, at ease...
- Negative and undesirable nonverbal messages include:
  - Evasive, weak, immature, boorish, remote, unprofessional, inexperienced, arrogant, unapproachable, standoffish, hard to work with, easily rattled under pressure, uncertain, incompetent...
- Nonverbal, positive "rapport builders":
  - Use consistent eye contact.
  - Be aware of facial expressions.
  - Optimize every aspect of your appearance.
  - Make your gestures and motions work for you. Gestures should be large and deliberate; they must not appear frantic, disorganized, or nervous. Use sufficient gestures to maintain interest and emphasize important points.

To accomplish positive and effective nonverbal communication, practice the following as you rehearse:

- Remove everything from your pockets that can make noise (phone, coins, keys, cellophane wrappers, pens or marker tops that click, nail clippers).
- Walk to the podium with assurance, eagerness, and confidence. The audience starts to judge you the moment you first move.
- Allow your natural body language to speak openly and sincerely (eyes, face, arms, hands, smile, posture).
- Do not pace, sway, slump, or lean on available furniture, but you do not need to be cemented in place as you present. When you move, it must be purposeful and deliberate, which will prevent distracting nervous motions, such as rocking, dancing, pacing, and fidgeting.

- Use eye contact to your best advantage as the most important and immediate form of nonverbal feedback.
  - Smile with your eyes! Bright eyes show that you are excited about your message, and this quickly engages the audience.
  - Avoid the tendency to speak only to the person in the audience who holds the most senior position and ignore the others, leaving them feeling slighted.
  - Speak to, and make eye contact with, everyone.

When making eye contact, don't move from one person to another too quickly. Maintain eye contact long enough to complete a sentence or make a point.

Effective Use of Your Hands

"What do I do with my hands?" is probably the most common question people ask. When presenting, many people cut their hands out of the action by adopting one of several common "frozen-speaker" positions, as shown in Table 4.2. These become the "home base" for their hands as they may gesture a bit or point to the screen, and each time return to the same position.

Table 4.2   "Frozen-Speaker" Positions to Avoid

"Frozen Speaker" Position	Description
	Both hands gripped together and covering the groin
Figure 4.2 Fig Leaf	
	Hands gripped behind the back (Like military at-ease position)
Figure 4.3 Reverse Fig Leaf	

"Frozen Speaker" Position	Description

Figure 4.4 Mortician

or

Hands gripped together or fingertips touching at the chest level

Figure 4.5 Concert Singer

"Frozen Speaker" Position	Description

Both arms hanging stiffly away from both sides

Figure 4.6 Gunfighter or Gorilla

Hands in pockets

Figure 4.7 Casual

"Frozen Speaker" Position	Description

Hands on both hips

Figure 4.8 Challenger

Hands firmly holding onto a lectern, chair, pointer, or papers

Figure 4.9 Paper Death Grip

"Frozen Speaker" Position	Description

Figure 4.10 Chair Death Grip

Hands and arms crossed over the chest

Figure 4.11 Crossed Arms

"Frozen Speaker" Position	Description

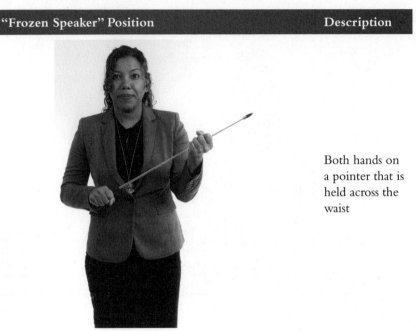

Both hands on a pointer that is held across the waist

Figure 4.12 Tightrope Walker

Effective Use of Your Face

A natural smile is very effective and connecting. It provides marvelous reinforcement when used at the right times. Excessive somberness, frowns, and scowls will alienate the audience; so will excessive grinning and unnatural smiles.

Consider a natural conversation with good friends. Use the same facial expressions in your presentation that you would in that conversation.

Smile with your eyes. Friendly eyes are very engaging, make your audience feel at ease with you, and convey a positive, upbeat, and honest attitude.

Effective Use of Your Body: Posture and Gestures

Your body should send the signals of control, energy, animation, enthusiasm, and confidence (see Figures 4.13, 4.14, and 4.15):

- Stand straight and erect, without slumping.
- Keep your shoulders relaxed, not tense.

- Don't pace, sway, rock, or dance.
- Avoid set patterns of motion that repeat themselves and become monotonous.
- If there is any piece of furniture nearby, resist the urge to lean on it.
- Sustain your energy.

Consider the tips in Table 4.3 regarding how an audience reacts to a speaker.

Table 4.3	Audience Reactions to a Speaker's Nonverbal Cues

If a presenter is…	The audience will…
Confident, relaxed, enthusiastic	Be eager to listen, hear the message, enjoy the presentation
Tense	Be uncomfortable, worry for you, miss the message
Stiff, flat	Tune out, drift off

Figure 4.13	Be Friendly!

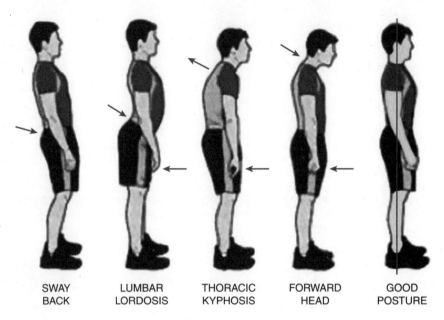

SWAY
BACK

LUMBAR
LORDOSIS

THORACIC
KYPHOSIS

FORWARD
HEAD

GOOD
POSTURE

Figure 4.14   Posture Counts

Figure 4.15   Be Yourself!

Connect with the Audience Emotionally and Psychologically

Unless You Connect, You Are Just Another Team

You carefully selected content to best represent and differentiate your team. You can leverage this unique, excellent content by delivering it with distinction. To do so, you must connect with the customer.

Making a strong connection with the customer is key to believability, and this is crucial to winning the contract. Remember, your primary objective is to make sure the customer thoroughly understands your message and is convinced your team is the best to deliver what they need. Identifying common ground that you share with the customer and emphasizing key points on which you both agree is the first step to making a positive connection.

Verbal choices that help you come across as believable include:

- Natural English, not "proposal speak."
- Similes and analogies to help them visualize.
- Stories and anecdotes to connect on a personal level.
- Using the customer's preferred terminology, references, examples, hot buttons, and experiences to help establish and reinforce your connection.

Key ingredients of a presentation or speech that convey the most believability and credibility:

- **Verbal** – Select words and key phrases that convey the credibility of your organization. Your voice also has an impact. The following elements have the greatest influence:
    - Intonations
    - Pace
    - Pitch
    - Projection
    - Conviction

- **Visual**—What the customer sees is what they believe they will get. Be aware of:
  - Expression
  - Gestures
  - Body
  - Mannerisms
  - Posture
- **Command**—This includes:
  - Knowledge
  - Skills
  - Resources
  - Understanding of their business
  - Commitment
  - Driven by their success
  - Your value and benefit to them for this project
  - Your perceived confidence and passion for the challenge

Emotional and psychological connection with the customer is unique to your team and your knowledge of the customer's sensitivities, preferences, likes, and dislikes. It can be a powerful positive discriminator, or a large, potentially disastrous distraction if it doesn't happen.

Emotional and psychological connection requires that you infuse the presentation with positive emotional triggers. Determining when, how, and why to infuse these triggers is critical. All pathways to emotional connection are not equally effective.

Negative emotions create barricades between your team and the audience, while positive emotions enhance persuasion. As carefully as you attended to content and scripting, you must be equally attentive to your emotional and psychological effect on the customer. Without a strong, credible, unique connection to the audience, you are just another team doing just another presentation.

Remember the old adage, *"I hear and I forget; I see and I remember; I do and I understand."* Connecting with and engaging your customer *involves* them to help them better understand you, your team, and your capabilities.

There are many techniques you can use to establish rapport with your audience and keep them engaged. For any of them to be effective, you must first analyze and understand your audience.

Questions to ask yourselves about your audience:

- Are they technical, nontechnical, or a mix of both?
- Do they have experience with you and/or your competitors?
- If an incumbent contractor is in place, do they want a change or prefer to maintain the status quo?
- Are they willing to accept change?
- Do they want an evolutionary or revolutionary change to their project?

These impact the emotional triggers that may be effective or have a negative effect. Be aware of both potential effects when connecting with the customer.

Following are some of the different types of techniques you can use for connecting.

Attention Getters

- Create surprise. Although there's no logical reason to believe that a presenter who starts with a surprise will deliver a more valuable presentation, a surprise will get the audience's attention and interest. Make sure the surprise is positive!
- Evoke curiosity. Include a bold claim or a startling statistic to get the audience's attention, and then follow up with the explanation and evidence. Your discriminators should all fall into this category. Use them to your advantage.

Emotional Aspects

- Determine emotional themes and points that will resonate with the audience, and decide when and how they should be presented. Essentially, these are the customer's hot buttons. A great deal of your time has been spent understanding what's important to the customer and the audience. Use this knowledge to your advantage by integrating these points into your presentation.

- Carefully select words for emotional emphasis where you can be absolutely certain of the customer's positive response, based on your thorough knowledge of your customer.
    - Would they respond more favorably to, "Our program manager has done a great job with the data center," or, "Our program manager started with a data center that was disorganized and overcrowded and transformed it into a center that is reliable to XX% and scalable for data and housing additional equipment." Be keenly aware that the customer may not want to hear that their data center was disorganized and overcrowded. Never ever call your customer's baby ugly!
- Model the emotion you want to elicit with your delivery technique: your tone, volume, pace, inflection, and body language. Great delivery magnifies emotions; poor delivery nullifies them.
- Connect with your eyes. Meaningful eye contact is about connecting with one person at a time. Your eyes will reflect your emotion. You want the customer's eyes to mirror your emotion. That's connection!

Stories, Colorful References, Visuals, and Physical Aspects

- Use analogies and metaphors to make your presentation more interesting and connect with the customer by tapping into their emotions that surround a particular topic. This is effective only when you are sure of the customer's feelings, and once again, the customer's hot buttons and key requirements play a very important role.
- When used selectively, stories are often the most memorable components of a presentation and the quickest way to achieve the greatest connection with the customer. As with all content, stories must

follow the flow of the presentation, fit naturally, reinforce your message, and be directly applicable to the opportunity at hand.

- Connect through visuals. If appropriate, embed photos or short videos in some of your charts. Going back to the data center example, showing a photograph of a well-organized center will have more impact than words alone.
- Eliminate physical barriers. Get out from behind the podium or other furniture that may come between you and your ability to connect. At the same time, beware of invading the audience's personal space, or getting uncomfortably close to them. There must be respectful separation, but not barriers to connection.

Be authentic and be honest. To share an emotion, you need to feel it. Your goal is to create in the customer's mind the same passion you feel about a topic or situation.

Your ability to make a sincere connection also requires your awareness that tripping a negative emotional issue can cost you the contract. Situations where you aren't familiar with the audience are potentially dangerous. Be careful not to say something or use a gesture that accidentally triggers an unintended emotion. If you're lucky, the misstep will provoke unexpected laughter; if you're not lucky, it may deeply offend the audience to a degree that they tune you out completely.

As you plan and work to make a connection with the customer, avoid using "I," "me," or "my." Instead, use words that include everyone in the room: "let's," "together," "we," and "our."

Convince them you understand what they are facing, and that you want to solve it by working with them. Personalize your message by using phrases such as:

- "We understand your biggest concern is…"
- "If we were in your situation…"
- "We can relate to your challenge of…"

Weave these phrases described in the "Using Content and Delivery to Connect" section in Chapter 3 into your delivery to help you connect with your audience. This will help you forge a powerful, positive relationship with the customer.

- "... which we recognize is very important to you."
- "... which we know is one of your key objectives."
- "Let me illustrate this with something we know is important to you..."
- "You will experience a major improvement in... or satisfy your major objective of... when we..."
- "... which will make your life easier by..."
- "... which, from your perspective, will..."
- "The reason why this is critical to you is..."
- "This is how you'll experience significant savings..."
- "How does this benefit you? The answer is..."
- "You might ask, "Why?" Well,..."
- "Here's why we feel this is essential to your needs..."
- "We believe this is vital to your customer because..."

Always remember that customers are continuously asking themselves:

- "Will these people come through for me?"
- "Will they meet my needs?"
- "Will they be committed?"
- "Will they work well together?"
- "Will they work well with me?"
- "Will they be responsive to our needs and priorities?"
- "Will they do quality work?"
- "Can I truly trust them?"
- "Can they relate to my challenges?"
- "Are they really what they claim to be?"
- "Will they be sensitive to my cost and schedule constraints?"

- "Would we be compatible" (in style, ethics, philosophy, character, motivation, goals, management, personality, culture)?

As you rehearse ways to connect with the customer to increase your win probability, consider the following:

- Genuine, natural enthusiasm, without being excessive, wins people over. The customer will respect you when they are convinced that you clearly believe in what you are saying.
- Be optimistic in your attitude toward your claims, your team, yourself, your capabilities, and working with the customer.
- Carefully watch the customer and adapt to their behavior. Watch how they are listening to you, and how they respond to you nonverbally. Adapt your delivery according to their reactions to the extent reasonable and feasible.
- A huge subconscious message that will affect the customer positively or negatively is the degree of teamwork they sense in all of the presenters toward each other. Assessing your ability to work together is one reason that customers require a formal oral presentation. They will see this (or not see it) in your handoffs to each other, your nonverbal support of each other, your references to each other, and your attitude, energy, and conviction toward each other.
- During the entire presentation, the customer will be observing every one of your team members, not just the presenter. They will consciously and subconsciously watch to see if you truly are a cohesive and unified team. Be aware of the signals that your team members are sending during each presenter's portion (see Figures 4.16 and 4.17). Every team member must be attentive and alert during the entire presentation!
- A sure way to blow your chances of being awarded the contract is by conveying an attitude of arrogance. Customers detest arrogance. Your challenge is to achieve a balance between confidence and humility. This can be difficult to do, but it is essential if you want to win.

Figure 4.16   Be Attentive Not Bored!

Figure 4.17   Body Language Counts

When you connect with the customer in a positive manner and they perceive you to be believable and credible, you make their decision to award you the contract an easy one. The entire time you are in the customer's facility you never stop selling, convincing, and persuading... gracefully promoting yourself, your ideas, your information, your team, and your company.

Customers from a broad range of market segments have used the following adjectives to describe oral presentation teams that capitalized on *Mastering the Art of Oral Presentations.* Use these as a checklist to help you determine the impact and effectiveness of your presentation style:

- Commanding
- Forceful presence
- Natural, sincere, real
- Creative
- Compelling
- Credible
- Professional

- Energetic
- Convincing
- Committed
- Persuasive
- Dynamic
- Logical
- Unified

Engaging — General Delivery Tips

Learn to Be Great from the Greats

Great presenters focus on the audience. They keep their messages simple and direct. They are well organized and professional. Their presentations flow smoothly and appear natural and effortless.

The principles described in *Mastering the Art of Oral Presentations* have been helping presentation teams achieve greatness for decades. As your team rehearses, consider the following summary of tips from our long and successful history.

Reminders

- All aspects of your formal oral presentation will be evaluated, even though your proposal evaluation instructions may say otherwise.

The customer will watch, judge, and evaluate everything that happens, psychologically and emotionally, consciously and subconsciously.
- Be crystal clear on your key points:
  - How will you make them stand out?
  - How will you reinforce them?
  - What else could you do to make sure the audience understands and retains them?
- Be sure your presentation will not create questions in the minds of your audience. Your presentation must offer solutions, not generate questions.
- For incumbents, beware of "incumbentitis" that can slip into tone, attitude, and countenance.
- Continually assess the effectiveness of your message focus areas:
  - Credibility
  - Reliability
  - Professionalism
  - Creativity and innovation
  - Thoroughness
  - Balance between confidence and humility
  - Honesty
  - Responsiveness

Your Professional and Personal Style and Energy

- Be yourself. Let your own natural personality show through. Yes, learn from others, borrow admired techniques and skills, but don't lose "you" in the process. New ideas should only enhance the genuine and unique you. Remember, this is similar to a job interview on stage. The customer needs to get to know the real you.
- Avoid a stiff, overly formal, canned delivery. That is not what they want to hear.
- Your delivery is the only vehicle you have to convey to them whether you have energy, passion, conviction, and commitment.
- Always remember to be humble but exude confidence.

- Everything you do and say should enhance the team's image and reputation.
- Channel nervousness into conviction, energy, and positive body language.

Customer Interaction

- Talk to your audience, never to your charts.
- Reference your team members, suppliers, and vendors occasionally during your presentation to reinforce support for each other and your ability to work together to achieve the best solutions for the customer.
- Help the customer understand your presentation without speaking down to them. Make it easy to follow your logic, explanation, and messages. A common saying among journalists and presenters states: "Never overestimate your audience's knowledge; never underestimate their intelligence." Prepare and present accordingly.
- Discreetly watch key customers for nonverbal cues during the presentation.

Timing

- Staying within your time limit is imperative. Anything exceeding your team's time limit is typically not scored and will degrade your evaluation.
- Monitor your pace: not too slow and not too fast.
- If you discover you are running short on time, you can omit some details without sacrificing too much of your message. For example, you could say, "Our key personnel meet or exceed your requirements." This will get you by, even though you would ideally point out the distinguishing skills and experience of your key personnel.

Team and Executive Interactions

- When you introduce or refer to key personnel in the course of the presentation, do not preface their titles with the word "proposed,"—for example, "proposed program manager." Saying, "[name] is our program manager" conveys greater confidence and assertiveness without being excessively presumptuous.

- As each new presenter begins, the audience may be looking down at their notes. Watch them for a moment and wait until they are looking at you before you begin speaking.
- Transitions from one presenter to the next must be seamless. This also demonstrates efficient teamwork to the customer.
- Don't walk away as you introduce or transition to the next presenter. Stay in position until the transition is complete, then walk to your seat.
- The presentation team is usually allowed and advised to have a senior executive such as the president, CEO, or executive vice president in attendance. If they are allowed to speak, the most important thing they should say in their one to two minutes is, "I give my full support and authority to [the leader of the project or program] and this team."
  - The customer is interested in "Is this company and team committed to me and the success of this project?" from the executive and the rest of their organization. The executive can also state that they are one email or phone call away from the program, and they will always be available to the customer.
- Somewhere in the presentation there should be a chart that shows a close organizational relationship among the executive, project lead, and customer.

Tools and Techniques

- If the speaker does not directly control charts, the person operating the remote control to advance the charts must be in sync with the presenter. They must have intimate knowledge of the content to deliver perfectly timed, seamless chart transitions.
- During your presentation avoid saying, "Next chart" to the person who is changing the charts. A small head nod is less obtrusive. With enough preparation and awareness, a head nod will be sufficient when one is needed.

- The podium restricts your movements and your ability to connect with your audience. Even if one is provided, gracefully avoid using it if you can.
- You may be required to use a microphone.
  - For speeches and formal oral presentations, a wireless system with a clip-on microphone is best for comfortable mobility. Position the microphone centrally on your body, not to one extreme side or the other. Because some microphones tend to be directional, ensure you do not talk over your shoulder when simultaneously pointing to a chart or a graphic.
  - Podiums and lecterns with built-in microphones, floor standing microphones, and large handheld microphones offer yet another challenge. Since they tend to be much more directionally sensitive than clip-ons, ensure the microphone is properly positioned relative to your mouth and hold this position while speaking.
  - If possible, practice using a microphone during your rehearsals if you know that one will be used in your final formal presentation or speech. Microphones are an exceptionally good speaking aid when used properly.

Using Props and Visuals

Don't Let Props and Visuals Take Control

Your presentation material complements your script, so your focus during orals should be on your delivery, not your charts. To help you effectively deal with presentation material, use the following practices:

- Tell your story using the chart, but never talking to the chart! Eye contact must be with the customer, not with your visual aids.
- Laser pointers have pluses and minuses. As a general rule, the minuses far outweigh the pluses. They generate too many distractions and

require significant skill coupled with a rock-solid hand to use them effectively. There are few things more distracting than a nervous hand causing a sensitive laser to appear unsteady on a screen. Use verbal pointers—for example, "the graph in the upper left corner."

- Do your best to stay out of the projection light.
- If you are using paper charts rather than projecting them, fold up a small corner at the bottom to ease page turning. Light pencil marks can be used to make "cheat notes" on paper chart margins that only you can see.

Practice, Practice, Practice

Practice Leverages Preparation to Create Success

The customer may initially be skeptical, cynical, pessimistic, or suspicious of you, your team, or your approach to solving their issues and concerns. To overcome any of their negative emotions, you must be genuine, honest, sincere, and accurate. You must answer their unspoken questions such as, "So what?" and "What's in it for me?"

In addition, be aware that the customer's contracting authority or legal counsel will instruct them beforehand to behave in a certain way during every presentation. This will likely include instructions not to engage with the presentation team, make facial reactions, show familiarity from the past, or ask spontaneous questions.

If you are an incumbent and have a good working relationship with the customer, don't be offended, disturbed, or surprised if you receive an unusually cool reception. When this happens it's usually because your customer has been "coached" by their contracts or legal team.

Many government customers go to great lengths to ensure that every single contractor is treated exactly the same. Doing this helps to avoid favoritism and makes sure the procurement is based solely on the content of the offer.

The compelling delivery of your presentation is the only way to prove to the customer that your team is in command of the required information, has the best solution, and is the one with whom they prefer to work. The only way to achieve a great delivery is to practice and rehearse over and over again.

The most effective way to rehearse is out loud, even if you practice alone away from the coach or other presenters. One way to improve delivery through independent practice is to rehearse in front of a mirror. Rehearsing out loud helps you:

- Eliminate words and phrases that you have difficulty pronouncing, minimize tongue twisters, and change anything that sounds awkward or cumbersome.
- Determine the appropriate length of phrases and sentences, and fine-tune your content (too short, too long, not necessary).
- Achieve appropriate pacing and accurate timing through the use of pauses, tonal emphasis, and rhythm changes.

The first walk-through is the first time you speak your part. This is the baseline that enables you to choreograph your presentation by priority and flow. After this exercise, you will be able to determine:

- What's right?—Keep it.
- What's wrong?—Drop it.
- What's confusing?—Clarify it.
- What's missing?—Add it.

The more familiar you are with your topic, the more you will perform with great confidence and competence. Your preparation will minimize nervousness and help you overcome interruptions, distractions, and other unanticipated events. The greater your preparation, the greater your chance is of securing the contract.

Dry Run Your Presentations

Practice Doesn't Make Perfect... Only Perfect Practice Makes Perfect
(Vince Lombardi)

Schedule time to conduct several formal, dry run presentations before making the presentation to your customer. In terms of preparation, there is no substitute for doing these, and they are an essential part of delivering a winning presentation.

Be careful not to overrehearse. This can generate confusion, tire the presenters, create team boredom, or promote a nonchalant presentation attitude. Your team may even start having a negative attitude about the entire process.

Plan your schedule to allow recovery time for the presentation team. Allow at least a day or two between formal rehearsals. Your goal is to get the team to "peak" right before the formal presentation to the customer. An experienced orals/speech coach knows how to make this happen, and their expert advice should be integrated early into your planning process.

Informal Dry Run

An informal dry run encompasses every aspect of the formal presentation in terms of charts (format, content, projection), presenter delivery, timing, and a mock Q&A session. It should be conducted by the presentation team under the guidance and tutelage of a professional orals coach. Informal dry runs must be done repeatedly (with planned breaks for recovery) until the team is satisfied that the final product and production meet all requirements—both yours and your customer's.

Formal Dry Run

Formal dry runs emulate, in every way possible, exactly how the presentation will be delivered to the customer. They are analogous to formal dress rehearsals in the entertainment business.

Formal dry runs use all elements of the informal dry run and add the following:

- All presenters wear exactly the same clothing that they will wear in the presentation to the customer.
- Entry into the presentation room, presenter seating, and exit out of the room is done exactly as it will be with the customer present.
- A mock audience is assembled to emulate the customer's evaluation team exactly as they will be represented in the formal presentation.
  - The mock audience will comprise the same number of individuals, with the domain knowledge required to perform a thorough evaluation of the presentation.
  - They will be intimately familiar with the procurement and the customer.
  - They should be capable of generating their own questions and qualified to determine if the answers are acceptable.
  - Ideally, they will also be familiar with how formal oral presentations are conducted and evaluated.

Master's Tip: Graciously Accept Constructive Criticism from Others, But Make the Final Decisions Yourself

Everybody wants to help you succeed, and you'll receive many suggestions for improvement (especially from reviewers and review committees). Suggestions for improvement frequently mean recommendations to add material. Respectfully accept any and all inputs—you may even get a great thought from a surprising source—but be very selective about which, if any, you accept.

No one knows the customer or the requirements better than you and your team do. So, discuss each input and select only those that add real value to your presentation. Stay on point and remain focused on the important issues. Don't get bogged down in minutia or items that detract from your major points.

- The presentation room should be arranged exactly as you believe the customer's facilities are arranged. Use the same presentation/ projection equipment and audio system that will be used with the customer.
- Timing is crucial and requires a great deal of practice.
  - Assign someone to keep the exact time of every presentation segment.
  - Almost always there is an exact amount of time specified for your presentation by the customer, and overrunning the time allotted is a very big negative.
  - Build in some margin; do not plan to use every available minute. It's much better to use a bit less time than to overrun.
  - An overrun will irritate your audience and could adversely affect your chances for an award.
- Never allow interruptions during the formal dry run. Instruct your mock audience to remain silent during the presentation, including the mock Q&A period. Ask them to write down their questions or comments and save them for a period of discussion and constructive criticism that will take place after the entire formal exercise is complete.

Master's Tip: "Perfect Practice" Equals Success

As the great coach of the Green Bay Packers National Football League team profoundly stated, "Practice doesn't make perfect. Perfect practice makes perfect." Indeed, Mr. Vince Lombardi knew what he was talking about. There is nothing more important than perfect practice. Practice perfectly and then do it again. Walk into your formal briefing with the customer knowing that you are well prepared and well rehearsed. Be confident that you will be as good as you can possibly be. Be confident that you will win!

Create a Mock-Up Presentation Room

Eliminate Surprises and Create Confidence

Understanding the physical space in which the presentation will take place will help you prepare to perform with confidence in that environment. Once you know the presentation location, the team will need to create a mock-up of the actual room to use during the final days of rehearsal. This will require accurate intelligence on dimensions, size, shape, layout, doors, windows, lighting, equipment, and anything else in or around the room that may affect the presentation. You can use masking tape on the rehearsal room floor to represent the room's dimensions and fixed furniture.

Determine, re-create, and prepare as follows:

- Is there enough lighting? Can it be adjusted? Where are the switches? Are they accessible and convenient?
- Are there blinds, shades, covers, drapes, or curtains on the windows? Can they be adjusted? How? Where? Who does it? Are they on a timer? Can you anticipate the sun's position during your presentation? Compensate for glare?
- Are there ceiling lights that could potentially shine onto your projection screen?
- Where are the electrical outlets? Do they work? Can you access them conveniently? Are they controlled by a switch?
- Are your equipment cords and cables long enough?
- Where is the thermostat? Can it be adjusted? Is there a blower that comes on unexpectedly? How loud is it?
- Will a microphone be used? If so, what kind?
- Is the sound system prone to blasts, shrieks, squeals, etc.?
- Is there piped-in sound or music from another room? Can it be turned off? How? Where? Who? Is there ambient noise that can be controlled, or for which the team will have to adjust?
- Does the projection table or desk have enough room for your chart projector?

- If the room has its own projector, are your hardware, software, and cables compatible with it? Who will set up the interface? Do you know the location of the on-off switch and other controls?
- What is the size of the projection screen? Will your charts display effectively?
- Is there a raised platform?
- Is there a permanent lectern?
- Are the chairs fixed in their positions?

The more intelligence you can gather, the fewer surprises you will experience.

Prepare for Common and Uncommon Events

Don't Let Murphy Win!

As Murphy was fond of saying, "If something can go wrong, it will." Part of your job is to prepare for every possible issue that could impact your presentation. Review and discuss the following common and uncommon events with the team, and determine how you will react should any of them occur. This is a long list, but know that every one of these things (and others) have happened in the past!

Personal

- Someone gets sick and can't make the presentation.
- Someone gets sick before the presentation starts.
- Someone gets sick during the presentation.
- Burps and hiccups.
- Sore throat.
- Speaker needs to blow their nose during the presentation and has no tissue.
- Problems with contacts or glasses.
- Need water and none is available in room.
- Overly stressed presenter.

- Extreme nervousness.
- Sweating while giving presentation.
- Need to go to restroom during orals — while not presenting.
- Need to go to restroom during orals — while presenting.
- You get desperately hungry or thirsty during the orals.
- A pant zipper is down.
- Dry mouth.
- Upset stomach, "gas" attack, or diarrhea.
- Cold/sniffles.
- Allergic reaction to medication.
- Sudden loss of voice.
- Clothing stain.

Presenter Errors

- Presenter goes blank.
- You state something incorrectly or make a mistake and you know it.
- You state something incorrectly or make a mistake and others on team pick it up.
- Internal timekeeper difficulty.
- Someone loses their place during a presentation.
- You are way over time allotment at end of first hour.
- You are way over your time allotment at end of second hour.
- Mental block.
- You notice a distraction by the current presenter that you know has to be a distraction to audience.
- Someone oversleeps and shows up late.

Challenges During Presentation

- A question is asked by the customer at the wrong (or unanticipated) time.
- A customer answers a cell phone.
- Significant, unexpected customer visitor joins the briefing after it starts.

- Customer directs a question at someone other than the presenter.
- Customer spills their drink.
- Customers start talking or whispering with each other.
- A customer points out an error on your chart or charts.
- Customer wants to caucus.
- One of your key people falls asleep.
- A customer falls asleep.
- One of your key people starts to cough uncontrollably.
- A customer starts to cough uncontrollably.
- Person who could/should respond to a question is not present.
- There is a fire drill.
- Presentation room becomes very hot or cold.
- Cell phone or pager rings.
- One of your team members' chair squeaks.
- Fire alarm, earthquake, or other emergency

Logistics

- Your luggage is lost.
- Suit doesn't fit or is left at the cleaner's or tailor's.
- Presentation room is different from what was arranged and planned for.
- Furniture setup has changed.
- You misplace the directions and address of the presentation location.
- Someone has car trouble.
- Traffic delays someone.
- Missing equipment.

Technical

- Power goes out.
- Laser pointer breaks.
- Microphone doesn't work, goes dead, or generates ear-piercing feedback.
- The projector bulb burns out or the large-screen display fails during your presentation.

- Ceiling lights shine directly onto the screen.
- Projectors have no obvious on/off switches.
- Equipment cords are about five feet too short.

Materials

- Chart is out of order.
- Lost handouts.
- Graphics packed in your luggage are lost in transit.
- You forget your laptop, and it has the charts in it.

Murphy's Law, also known by engineering students as "The Fourth Law of Thermodynamics," is alive and well! As it is typically stated, "Anything that can go wrong, will go wrong." The perceived perversity of the universe has long been a subject of comment, and precursors to the modern version of Murphy's Law are not hard to find — for example, the centuries-old German phrase "Die Tücke Der Dinge," which means "the perverseness of things" or "the treachery of things."

Here's a true story of one presenter's nightmare becoming a reality:

A young aerospace project manager (PM) was called upon to formally present an exciting new technology and product development plan to a very high-ranking DoD executive and several General Officers at the Pentagon. The presentation was to be conducted in the executive's office and last no more than 20 minutes.

Needless to say, a great deal of preparation work went into the presentation and it followed the guidance presented in this book, with one exception — there was no backup presenter for the young PM at the Pentagon. Standing outside of the executive's office with his boss's boss, the young PM began to feel genuinely physically sick. He started sweating, felt clammy, and was slightly nauseated. Nevertheless, the executive's office door opened right on time and the presentation started.

About 10 minutes into the presentation, the young PM knew that he was about to vomit. There was no doubt about it — it was going to happen and it was going to happen very quickly. In a quandary about where to relieve himself (and time was clearly of the essence), he quickly ran to the executive's desk, grabbed a trashcan, and used it to contain the plentiful vomitus.

The executive immediately called for a break and asked the young PM if he felt that he could compose himself in a few minutes and continue. Of course the answer was yes, and that's exactly what happened. Restarting the presentation, the young PM very soberly stated, "I sincerely apologize for the unscheduled break and hope that you will all understand why I needed one."

A hearty laugh followed, and the presentation was on again. In good nature, following the presentation, every single attendee gave the quick-thinking young presenter a pat on the back, and the presentation was, indeed, a total success. The young PM spent several days in bed recovering from the flu, and the special project moved forward.

This is only one stunning example of countless presentations that have experienced near-surrealistic events before or during the presentation session. The moral of this story: Try to anticipate and prepare for everything!

Question and Answer Sessions

Practice Your Process — Rely on Your Program Manager

The question and answer session (Q&A) is often designed to provide more information than just the obvious answers to the questions. For example, long after an award had been made, the winning team asked the customer if they had provided the right answers in their Q&A. The reply surprised them: The customer was more interested in seeing how the team handled the questions than in the actual answer content. This is often the case.

Yes, there will be certain clarifications and specific answers that the customer needs to hear, but there is no doubt that the Q&A phase clearly demonstrates to the customer how you will function as a team.

They will be able to watch your program manager lead the team. They will see how you share information and unite your capabilities to come up with answers.

The orals presentation is formal and rehearsed, but the Q&A is spontaneous and "real-time." There is no way to fake it. You can easily lose the job based on the Q&A even if your formal presentation was flawless and exceptional.

Do not become cavalier or overly confident during the Q&A. This is a time to be very serious, very thoughtful with your answers, and most importantly, very respectful of your customer's questions. It is a unique opportunity to truly demonstrate the dynamics, camaraderie, competence, and synergy of your team to your potential customer.

Use the following guidelines for your Q&A session.

Planning and Preparing

- Plan and maintain a formal response structure.
- Let the program manager take the lead and direct the questions to the appropriate team member for two primary reasons:
  - Increased efficiency.
  - To demonstrate the program manager's leadership and the team's support and responsiveness to it.
- Be ready with backup data. This will go beyond what was provided during the actual presentation and will help you clarify and answer a question while reinforcing in the customer's mind your excellent preparation.
- Identify the best chart makers from within the team who can be prepared (if really needed) to generate spontaneous charts or graphics to explain an answer to a question.
- Be prepared to use phrases like these to reply to questions:
  - "That is an understandable concern…"
  - "I appreciate why you are asking that question."
  - "We have asked ourselves that same question…"
  - "Did that answer your question?"

- A brief, relevant illustration, example, or story can help provide a convincing answer that will establish a connection with the customer. Prepare some examples/stories that can further illustrate your value proposition when given the opportunity during Q&A.
- The customer has an amazing sixth sense about asking you to explain the one thing in a busy chart that you don't fully understand. Be obsessive in your preparation.

Listening

- Listen intently to the entire question without interrupting.
- While the customer is asking the question, listen to the content (what is actually being asked) and listen for the intent (the actual meaning behind the question).
- Listen with your eyes and your ears: watch for their nonverbal cues.

Reacting

- Never, under any circumstances, lose your composure or even appear to be losing your composure.
- Keep your sense of humor.
- Don't ever divulge or show any negative verbal or nonverbal feelings about the question. Always stay upbeat, positive, and engaged.
- During the entire Q&A, whether you are the person answering or part of the support team, make sure your nonverbal communication does not contradict the verbal messages being delivered.
- Be extremely attentive and alert during the entire Q&A.
- Don't develop your answer halfway into their question. This could result in misunderstanding their entire question and indicate that you have tuned them out.
- You want the customer to see you as thoughtful, careful, and thorough. Never "shoot from the hip." Never fake it. Never feel pressured into providing incomplete or poorly phrased answers.

- Give your complete undivided focus and attention to the person asking the question.
- Be honest, positive, concise, and pleasant.

Answering Questions

- Before responding to a question, listen carefully and make sure you thoroughly understand it.
- If you don't understand the question, feel free to ask for clarification. Don't ever try to guess its real meaning.
- Acknowledge the question first before answering, for example, "That's a good question," "I'm glad you asked," or "Let me be sure that I understand what you are asking." Then rephrase or restate the question before answering it, unless this would be clearly unnecessary and redundant.
- Use the customers' names whenever possible.
- Answer the question completely, yet concisely. Avoid long, confusing, overly complex answers. You have already given your presentation. Don't start making a presentation about a whole new subject.
- At the end of your answer, ask the person who asked it if you answered their question.
- If there are factual errors or any fact-based misunderstandings, correct them immediately and clearly. Ensure the correct data is thoroughly understood by all.
- Answer all questions directly, courteously, and accurately without dodging or sidestepping the question.
- If you don't know the answer, look to your team for support. If it's clear that no one knows the answer, don't be afraid to say, "I don't know, but I'll get back to you shortly with an answer."
- Yes and no answers can often be seen as overly simplistic, or even evasive. Rambling is also counterproductive, but always provide a complete and adequate response.

- If a questioner points out an error that was made earlier, thank that person, accept and acknowledge it, and move on.
- If someone agrees with what you have said, simply thank that person, and move on.
- Never reply, "No comment."
- Never say, "Off the record…" Everything that is said is *always* on the record.

Leveraging Opportunities

- Take advantage of opportunities that certain questions will provide you by including a key point or discriminator from your presentation. Here is your chance to give it an additional punch by reminding your audience of your discriminator as you tie it into your answer to their question.
- Use some of your answers to intentionally clarify a portion of your presentation that you feel your audience missed or didn't fully grasp.
- If there is a question you were hoping they would ask, occasionally it is appropriate to add, at some point during the Q&A, "You may have been wondering about…"
- In your answer, try to refer to the solicitation and what it asks for. This not only provides the answer, but also shows that you are familiar with the requirements. It lets them know that you are diligent and have paid close attention to their requirements.

Remember, the Q&A does far more for the customer than hearing your answers. It allows them to observe and predict how you will work with them in the future, when you win the contract.

Many an orals competition has been lost because of poorly handled Q&A techniques. On the other hand, the Q&A can be an opportunity to redeem yourself from an earlier mistake, or a poor performance. At the very least, it can enhance and reinforce your earlier presentation, especially in areas in which you performed well.

Sample Questions Your Customer May Ask You

Being Well Prepared Means Anticipating the Questions That Your Audience May Ask

Time Spent Preparing Answers to Potential Questions Is Time Well Spent

As part of your preparation process, get some smart, knowledgeable people to develop your own comprehensive list of questions that you anticipate will be asked. Develop several hundred questions to use during your rehearsal process. When you perform your rehearsal before mock customers, encourage them to ask these questions. And remember, there is no such thing as a "dumb question."

This list is by no means complete, however, it does provide questions that are frequently asked by customers both during and after a presentation.

Technical

- You have proposed a technology insertion approach that will improve performance and drive down our operating cost. What will you do if this technology is not yet available when you need it?
- The tool that you are proposing to use is proprietary property of our existing contractor. It will not be available to use on this contract. What is your plan to address this issue?
- Can you give more specifics on the remote support and upgrade? How would this work?
- Can you be more specific on how the system works?
- Are you proposing any special tools that will be needed to do this job? Are they included in your price? Are they proprietary to your company?
- Are commercial off-the-shelf products all that are needed for this subsystem? Will they interface with the highly customized systems we have in place today?

Schedule

- Your schedule seems aggressive. Please tell us how you will accomplish all of the required tasks in the timeframe that you've defined for us.
- What will you do if we direct you to compress the project schedule by 20%?
- How will you manage work assignments when you are given multiple tasks that are all categorized as "high priority?"
- What will you do if the vendor's equipment isn't delivered on time? We noted that it's on your schedule's critical path.
- What will you do if some of the equipment that we are providing to you does not arrive on time?

Clarification

- We don't understand how you can take this risk from high to low. Can you please explain your approach in more detail?
- Could you describe your concept for conducting project and evaluation reviews in more detail?
- I didn't understand the relation between X and Y. Could you clarify this?
- What do you mean by verified and validated capability?
- Give an example of your phased deployment concept.
- What do you mean by _____?
- You claim to be world class! Exactly what does that mean and how do you justify this claim?

Money/Ethics/People

- We noted an inconsistency in the pricing information between your written proposal and this presentation. Which is correct?
- How will you handle the situation if one of our users approaches you and tells you to hire a certain company or individual?
- In this era of tight budgets, how will you address reduced funding on this procurement? How will you manage the workforce in this situation? How will you handle a reduction in workforce?

- Your project lead has indicated that retirement is fast approaching. What is your plan to replace this key individual? Are the other key people committed to our project for its duration?
- In the event you are awarded this contract, how do you plan to deal with the losing, disgruntled incumbent and ensure a smooth transition?

Chapter 5

Formal Presentation Day

*Demonstrate Your Competence,
Credibility, Confidence
and Commitment*

F ormal Presentation Day is the culmination of all your preparation. During the weeks preparing for orals, you evaluated your
team, the customer, and the competition. You carefully selected
and prepared your presentation package and script. You practiced and
rehearsed alone and with your team.

If you weren't an expert in your subject area before this process,
you are now. You have become the expert in your area for your team.
No one else, including the customer, knows your material, rationale,
and supporting evidence better than you. You have every reason to feel
relaxed and confident.

However, everyone has situations that make them nervous, and
some of us are more nervous than others about presenting to a

small group or a large audience. It's natural to have butterflies. Your goal is to get them to fly in formation!

Remember that nervousness is your friend. It is energy. It is essential for success. Channel your nervous energy into animation, conviction, and passion for your message.

Eleanor Roosevelt, former first lady of the United States, gave this wise advice: *"You gain strength, courage and confidence by every experience in which you look fear in the face. You must do that which you think you cannot do."*

Dealing with Nervousness and Distractions

Get the Butterflies to Fly in Formation

The most successful antidote for nervousness is ample preparation. Too often people spend way too much time worrying and fretting, instead of putting that time into more preparation and rehearsal. Lack of preparation will add to your nervousness. Focus your energy and efforts on what you want the customer to learn and understand, instead of worrying about yourself. The more prepared you are, the less nervous you will be. Preparation promotes confidence.

Interestingly enough, the small things that we are frequently most concerned about (that contribute to unnecessary nervousness and worry) don't really matter much because the audience rarely notices or cares about them. An example of this is the frequent worry of, "What do I do with my hands?" If this truly concerns you, then let your hands go naturally to their default position, the place where they naturally are when you aren't using them. Just let your hands go there and forget about them. The same applies to your feet.

One technique to help reduce nervousness is to identify what you are specifically anxious about. When you have done that, try to separate yourself from the anxiety and then logically and objectively analyze the cause for those concerns, worries, or fears. Does it result from lack of practice, lack of preparation, uncertain content, mind blanks, knee or hand shaking, or something else? There are tricks, crutches, hints, and solutions for addressing each of these issues.

As you discover the sources of your nervousness, your coach will help you address each one. Reassuring yourself that you are, in fact, well prepared can often eliminate the majority of your fear. The more you prepare and practice, the more confident you will become. In parallel, you will reduce your nervousness and your fears.

To further help you deal with fear, make a list of everything that could hypothetically go wrong during your presentation, and then rationally determine the odds of each of these things actually happening. You will realize the majority of your fears are extremely unlikely occurrences. If you feel there is a high likelihood of some of these happening, then for those few, identify contingent actions to mitigate them. Mentally or physically rehearse the scene of these occurring, so that if they do occur, you will be prepared to deal with them.

Since nervousness while presenting is a common challenge, *Mastering the Art of Oral Presentations* has collected a variety of fear-management techniques that have proven useful for controlling nerves to prevent them from controlling the presentation.

- Have a strong, well-founded personal commitment to your subject.
- Be convinced that what you have to say is valuable to the customer and their decision-making process.
- Be assured that you are an expert on your topic. You are the best person to present this material.
- Remind yourself over and over that senior management believes that you are the best person to speak on this topic, or you would not have been asked to be part of the team. No one has the same experience, background, judgment, knowledge, education, and successes that you do.
- Spend ample time rehearsing the team member introductions.
- Knowing your first two phrases inside out will carry you through your initial nervousness and into a confident and comfortable flow.
- Once you get past the opening, your nervousness will dramatically subside.

- Many people experience nervousness about giving a presentation based upon their personal expectations of absolute perfection. Know and accept the fact that this is not going to happen. No one is perfect.
- If you make a mistake during your presentation, quite often it will not be noticed, so don't broadcast it. If you must correct the error or provide clarification, do so simply and quickly. Don't belabor it. Let the situation go. Your teammates must not react to the mistake either, or they will bring unnecessary attention to it and detract from your presentation.
- If a genuine mistake is made or something goes wrong during the actual presentation, the audience will watch how you handle it as an indicator of how you will handle mistakes on the job. Take a brief time to compose yourself and resist the urge to correct or address the issue too quickly. Think fast (we're talking seconds here), but do think through the issue and decide how you will address it before proceeding. If you are facing a complex issue or problem, you might say something like, "Please give me just a moment to think through this issue and ensure that I give you the correct answer."
- Understand the value of physical movements in coping with fear. Excess nervousness is often the result of uncontrolled and unchanneled physical energy. Well-proven techniques to deal with this include:
  - Before presenting, squeeze your thumb against your index finger in an isometric fashion, subtly, for the count of ten. Repeat this with each of the other fingers against the thumb.
  - Tighten various muscle groups, and then relax them. Wiggle your toes, clench your fists, and discreetly perform other muscle isometrics. Do this subtly so that you do not appear silly.
  - Inhale deeply and slowly through your nose, exhale slowly through your mouth, and concentrate on your breathing. Repeat three times, and then smile.
- When you feel nervous, talk to the "friendly" faces in the audience first. As you gain more confidence during the course of your presentation,

you will be able to move to other faces as well, until you cover all the customers. Remember that feeling nervous can work to your advantage.

As you are mentally preparing to present, remind yourself to be more concerned about your audience than yourself. As you begin speaking, focus on your message, and not on how you sound or look. Remember how many times you have rehearsed with your teammates, how far you have come, and how well you have done in the past. At this point, no one is better prepared to present your material to the customer than you. Remember that nervousness is natural and normal, and if you don't have it to a certain degree, your presentation may not contain the vitality, energy, animation, and conviction that it needs.

Certain biological manifestations of nervousness, such as sweaty palms, dry throat and mouth, butterflies, shaky knees, are very normal. Believe it or not, they will decrease and even disappear when you ignore them and focus on your presentation. Forget your fear and deliver. If you are well prepared and well coached you will do a superb job. In fact, when you finish and look back on your presentation, you will be very pleasantly surprised at how well you have done.

Delivery Distractions

Common things can become major distractions to you, your team, and especially your audience during your presentation. Be aware of them, work to prevent them, and be prepared to mitigate them. Delivery distractions may include:

- Change, keys in pocket.
- Poor posture — slouching.
- Rocking.
- Verbal static: "Um," "uh," "and," "okay," and so on.
- Reading charts.

- Standing in projection light.
- Pointing across body (wrong arm).
- Fidgeting.
- A mobile phone ringing or vibrating.
- Twitches.
- Poor grammar.
- Offensive terms, swearing, cussing.
- Outside noises.
- Distracting behavior of team members during your presentation.
- Excessive use of slang.

Guidelines for Interacting with the Customer

Your Future Is in Their Hands

The customer is unquestionably in charge during your formal oral presentation. They will have been schooled by their contracting officers, legal department, and/or buyers on treating all presentation teams equally. They will have been instructed not to react either favorably or unfavorably during your presentation and Q&A session.

However, there will be time before and after your official presentation when you will be in a position to interact with the customers. In these situations, don't discuss the proposal. No matter how well you know the customers, this is the first time they will see you in your proposed position. Show them the utmost respect. Remember, a new contract equates to a new you.

Greet customers as they enter the room, firmly shake hands while looking the customer directly in the eyes, and introduce yourself (name and bid position) if necessary. Be polite and cordial to everyone. Introduce team members if appropriate. Introductions create the all-important first impression. Address customers according to their knowledge and position. Beware of making any of them feel left out and beware of condescension. Attend patiently and politely whenever a customer speaks. They hold your future in their hands!

Master's Tip: Smiling Eyes and a Firm Handshake Help Earn Credibility and Trust

When greeting individuals, always use a firm handshake, look the other person directly in the eyes, and smile. Smile with your eyes as well as your mouth. There are few things more unsettling and confidence eroding than being on the receiving end of a soft and unresponsive dead-fish handshake without eye contact and no smile.

You must convey confidence, honesty, and enthusiasm. There is no better way to do this than by giving a firm shake with smiling eyes that are filled with enthusiasm.

Formal Presentation Day Emergency Kit

Be Prepared for Murphy's Law

If you fail to prepare, you're prepared to fail. Prepare for the unexpected and make sure you're ready for anything that may happen. To help you be prepared, *Mastering the Art of Oral Presentations* recommends that you take the following items with you on Formal Presentation Day. At some point in our experience, an orals team has been exceedingly grateful that they brought each of these along.

Personal Hygiene

- Aspirin/pain relief tablets
- Cough drops
- Antacids
- Nondrowsy antihistamine (for allergy attack)
- Adhesive bandages
- Dental floss
- Toothpaste and travel-sized toothbrush
- Breath freshener spray/drops
- Tissues
- Deodorant
- Lip balm (for dry lips)
- Lemon hard candy (for dry mouth)
- Bottled water

Personal Appearance

- Makeup kit with basics (lipstick, blush, mascara, blemish cover-up, touch-up nail polish)
- Extra neutral-colored necktie

- Extra shirt/blouse
- Extra hosiery and/or under-wear
- Lint remover
- Sewing kit
- Safety pins
- Comb or brush
- Nail clippers/nail file/emery board
- Small scissors
- Small mirror

Tools

- Air freshener spray
- Tape
- Scissors
- Pens, pencils, highlighters, markers
- Notepad
- Sticky notes

Essential Backup Equipment to Take with You

If you have this equipment with you, you likely won't need it. But if you don't have it with you, you will definitely need it, so take it with you.

- Extra cords and original cords for all equipment.
- Two projectors.
- Extra bulbs and know how to replace them fast!
- Spare batteries for everything that requires batteries.
- Projector table.
- Memory stick with presentation materials carried in a separate car.
- Voltage adapter, if applicable.
- Flashlight.
- Extra "loaded" laptop.
- Tool kit.

Final Preparations

It's Your Day!

Many orals teams spend the night before their presentation at a hotel near the presentation location. This mitigates the impact of both traffic emergencies and foul weather. Regardless of whether or not you spend the night at a nearby location, check the weather forecast and be prepared.

Get a good night's sleep. Resist the urge to eat a big, heavy dinner or overindulge in any way. Being well rested and as sharp as you can possibly be is critical for success. There will be plenty of time for celebrating after you finish your presentation!

The day of your presentation, meet somewhere easy to find and arrive at the presentation location as a team. Turn off all mobile phones and personal electronic devices.

Be ready to start on time—do not be late! Arrive more than early enough to allow time for security/access requirements, setting up and testing all equipment, and distributing handouts.

Give yourself a pep talk before the presentation begins. Gather as a team and remind yourselves that your team is the best team for the job. You are the experts. You are prepared. Picture yourself presenting perfectly. Breathe deeply. Smile. You are supported by your teammates. You will perform well. Relax and enjoy the day—it will be one that you will never forget!

The After-Presentation Action Review

Capture Your Thoughts While They're Fresh in Your Mind

As soon as your presentation is complete, get your team together in a quiet place to objectively review what happened. Discuss and document the following items:

- Action items you may have taken that require follow-up with the customer. Assign one person to be responsible for coordinating the action response with the team. Assign individuals by name to specific action items.
- All questions that the audience/customer asked and how you answered each of these. Note if any of the written materials (charts, written proposal, etc.) are affected by the answers.
- General impressions that team members noted when they were not presenting.

- Feedback that individual customers may have provided during non-presentation times such as breaks, pre- or postmeeting talks, and so on.
- Errors on written materials.
- Lessons learned.
- If a follow-up written response of any kind is required of you, ensure that each response is reviewed with, and agreed upon, by the entire team. Also ensure that the response language is clear, well written, and error free.

Celebrate!

Celebrate Success with Your Presentation and Support Team

You have worked long and hard to get to this point; now it's time to celebrate. Never pass up the opportunity to celebrate major accomplishments such as completion of a rigorous oral presentation. Celebrations can be simple or extravagant affairs. Pick whatever best suits your team and acknowledge the hard work that everyone has put into making your big day a success.

By all means, don't forget to formally acknowledge all the supporting people who helped you out along the way. Be sure to include graphic artists, technical and management experts, administrative assistants, subcontractors, vendors, IT people, technicians, contributing superiors/executives, and anyone who made contributions. They will appreciate being recognized and enjoy the opportunity to celebrate your success right along with you.

Chapter 6

Real-Time Demonstrations–A Truly Special Experience!

Live Demonstrations Present New Challenges and Opportunities to Crush Your Competition

C ustomer requests for real-time demonstrations (demos) are becoming more and more commonplace. Technology has progressed to a point where many aspects of a product, network, subsystem, or complete system can be thoroughly demonstrated to and evaluated by the customer in near real-time. When customers ask for demonstrations, a significant amount of extra preparation and planning is required as a part of the presentation process. This section of *Mastering the Art of Oral Presentations* deals with the spe-

141

cial issues associated with real-time demonstrations that are integrated into the overall presentation process.

Understanding the Demo Requirements

Understand What Your Customer Is Looking for in a Live Demo and Thoroughly Address All Their Requirements and Concerns

When a customer asks for a demo, there is usually a very good reason and rationale for doing so. Clearly, there are many reasons that may motivate a customer's request for a live, real-time demo. The demo might address a particular operating feature that has high value to the customer, it might address a specific risk, it might serve to eliminate bidders that are not prepared to conduct a demo, or it might simply be to test the commitment and honesty of the seller.

An astute seller should attempt to find out what is driving the requirement for a demo and ensure the demo plan squarely addresses the motivating factor. The demo must also address every single requirement that is called out for it by the customer.

In some cases the customer will be very specific about what and how they expect to see demonstrated. When instructions are clear, your job is greatly simplified. A challenge comes when the customer says that a demo is desired, but there is no specificity on how it is to be accomplished. Let's look at each of these two cases and examine techniques used to successfully address each of them.

When Demonstration Requirements Are Clear

When demo requirements are clear, your task is greatly simplified, but conducting a successful demo is still a formidable task in many ways. You must (1) address every single demo requirement and (2) easily and clearly *convince the audience* that you have satisfied every requirement. These are two very different things!

One of the best ways to ensure you satisfy every demo requirement is to use a checklist. Making the checklist graphically visible to the customer is an important part of the demo and can be very effective when this technique is used properly.

For complex demos with many requirements, consider using a separate projector or large display screen on which you or an assistant simply check off each requirement as it is demonstrated. A large poster board and marker can also be used for this purpose if dual screens/large displays are not available. Another technique is to offer the customer a paper checklist that can be used to verify results while keeping the customer engaged and providing them with a written record of your performance.

There are many other ways to graphically show that your compliance with requirements has been satisfied. Whichever method you use to track and ensure compliance, you must be sure it's obvious to your customer that you have done so! Mechanically checking off a list or compliance matrix is meaningless unless your audience believes that you have actually demonstrated the capability.

When Demonstration Requirements Are Not Specified

When demonstration requirements are not specified, your demo task becomes much more difficult. It is now up to you and your team to decide how best to communicate and clearly show that you satisfy all of your customer's needs. Hot buttons, specifications, work tasks, risks, and derived requirements are all things that must be considered as you design your demo plan and presentation.

First, look at any requirements that the customer has provided or communicated to you in any way—for example, customer contact meetings, customer briefings, published documentation, and so on. Review the ones that are formally documented in the solicitation and carefully add any that you are convinced the customer needs but may not have been adequately or formally documented in the customer's solicitation package.

Once you have identified all these requirements, determine if you should demonstrate compliance with derived requirements. Derived requirements are generally associated with complex systems and are real requirements that are implied, or stem from, a higher-level requirement. For example, a formal requirement for a long range or high-speed vehicle may result in a derived design requirement for low-weight, high-efficiency, and/or increased power.

Derived requirements are generated by your team via engineering trade-offs and by applying proven system engineering design processes. When done well, demonstrating derived requirements shows you truly understand the customer's issues and have spent the time needed to thoroughly think and work through them. This is a great way to increase customer confidence in your approach and can easily distinguish you from your competition.

Master's Tip: Identifying and Understanding Derived Requirements Frequently Separates Winners from Losers

If you know that a demo will be required (or even if only high-level requirements are provided in the solicitation and a demo is not called for), starting work on derived requirements early can be very beneficial to both you and your customer. Conducting the rigorous system engineering studies and trades needed to generate derived requirements will frequently result in identification of design or implementation issues that were not previously thought of or considered. Obviously, bringing these to your customer's attention early in the procurement process is extremely beneficial and can easily save significant time, talent, and money in the future. As always, if there are unanticipated issues, unknowns, or surprises of any kind, it's best to know about them as soon as possible. If you are the team that brings significant issues forward early, your credibility will skyrocket with your customer.

The only word of caution is to not overplay or dwell too long on derived requirements that simply support well-understood, top-level requirements. Treat them as though they are "business as usual" for you and confidently be assured knowing that your evaluation score will rise.

Simple and Complex Demos—Either Way, Make Sure They "Get It"!

Simple demos should capitalize on obvious actions and tangible results. These types of demos are satisfying for the speaker and the audience as well. When conducting a simple demo, such as highlighting the properties and functions of a proven, commercially available product, don't rush it! Take your time and look for feedback from the audience.

Even when requirements are clear, complex demos require much more thought. Making your point and demonstrating compliance may require multiple steps or interrelated processes to arrive at the desired result.

When a demo is complex, it's imperative that every step leading up to the desired end state be explained and understood by the audience. The speaker must articulate what is happening and carefully guide the audience every step of the way. Furthermore, the speaker must tell why specific steps are being taken. Failure to do this may lead the audience to believe that artificial or less than complete tasks are being performed. This leads to doubt; don't let this happen.

Elimination of doubt is best worked out by thoroughly thinking through every step of the demo process and then using dry runs with a mock audience to provide feedback and suggestions for improvement. Do this over and over again until you and your audience are convinced that your demo is clear, easy to follow and understand, and compliant with every customer requirement.

Whether your demo is simple or complex, look for your audiences' heads nodding in the right direction, look for confirming smiles, and solicit positive audible feedback when it's appropriate. If you see confusion in the eyes of the audience, ask if your demo point was clear or if there are any questions. If need be, repeat your prior action taking into consideration what the sticking point was.

When things are going well and the audience is tracking right along with you, keep moving and don't dwell on obvious points that have been accepted by your audience. Going too slow is just as annoying as going too fast. Either way, you will lose your audience and the effectiveness of your demo will be diminished. Stay tuned into your audience's reactions to help you capitalize on this great opportunity to demonstrate your product as well as your differentiating value.

Getting from Good to Great with Deeper Insights — Discriminators, Risks, and Hot Buttons

Okay, so what's next? You've addressed all your customer's formally documented requirements as well as those that your team has derived. Now go back and look at your customer's hot buttons and concerns about risk. See if any of these items impact your demo plan and if there is a way for you to intelligently weave them into your presentation. Whenever this can be done, do it!

Experience has shown that demos frequently dwell on firm requirements alone and neglect less tangible factors (such as derived requirements) that are of interest to the customer. Conversely, demos that show real insight into customer issues, hot buttons, and risks are winners. Always look for, and demonstrate, features and items that are unique to your approach, show how you mitigate or eliminate risks, and focus on customer hot buttons. Optimizing your use of these techniques can help you support your customer's decision making and crush the competition.

The Demo Project Plan and Project Manager

Assign a Proven, Top-Notch Project Lead to Direct and Manage Your Live Demonstration

Given the complexity and many issues associated with conducting a live demo, it's a good idea to manage the demo as you would any other project. Assign a single project lead who is responsible for every aspect of your demonstration.

The project lead should *not* be one of the presenters. Keeping the project lead independent of a speaking role ensures that speakers focus on speaking and do not lose their concentration on this most important task. In addition to the major aspects of the demo, there are so many little details to manage that the project lead will likely have little time for anything else, much less worrying about a speaking role. And, the demo success depends on lots of little details just as much as it does on the major project tasks.

The project lead has many tasks to accomplish, such as:

- Building a demo schedule (in collaboration with the proposal and speaking team) with a critical path timeline supporting the actual presentation date with the customer.
- Development of demo cost estimate. This will be of particular interest to your higher-level management team since complex demos can be very expensive and significant funds may be required to resource a successful demo.
- Identification of all needed resources including people and equipment.
- Coordination with teammates, vendors, and suppliers.
- Arrangement of travel plans for people and equipment.
- Developing and managing contingency/backup plans for every element of the demo.
- Ensuring compliance with every demo requirement.

Teammate, Subcontractor, Vendor, and Supplier Support

Engage Every Member of Your Team and Make Them a Part of Your Winning Solution—Your Customers Will See Their Engagement as a Significant Strength

Your teammates, subcontractors, vendors, and suppliers play crucial roles in helping you develop and present a successful demo. Enlist their support and make them winning parts of your demo plans. The experience, knowledge, and skills these players bring to a demo are extremely valuable to you. Engage them in every aspect of planning, resourcing, and participating in your demo.

When you do this, your customer is very likely to notice and record this as a plus for your team. Customers view an integrated team as a success-oriented team that will work together to help address their issues and ensure overall project success. They will see that you know how to manage your team, optimize resources, take advantage of unique skills and knowledge, and minimize risks.

When using outside sources of any kind, protect yourself and your approach to winning the job. Put nondisclosure agreements in place, sign exclusive teaming agreements with your suppliers whenever possible, and ask for dedicated people to support you. In a world of competitive procurements, maintaining confidentiality is crucial. If you are not absolutely certain that your suppliers will honor your confidentiality agreement, find someone else to take their place. It's that important!

Visuals

Outstanding Visuals Enhance Your Presentation; Poor Visuals Can Destroy It

The most comprehensive demo in the world will fail if your customer cannot see what's happening or doesn't understand what's being shown. The ability to clearly show what's going on during a demo cannot be overstated. It is absolutely imperative that visuals be used expertly, are easy for everyone to see, and demonstrate compliance with requirements.

To start with, know the environment where the demo will be made: lighting, audience size, seating accommodations, and acoustics. Once these factors are understood, enlist the help of an audiovisual design professional. Don't use amateurs and don't make any assumptions. Thoroughly test your audiovisual solution exactly as it will be used in the formal demo. Use your solution as you conduct your dry runs. And by all means, make sure that all your equipment (and people) are backed-up at the location of the formal demo.

Planning for Success

Planning for Success Requires That You Expect the Unexpected

Expect the unexpected! Contingency planning is an important part of any mission. Your project lead must not only prepare for planned demo events but also work to anticipate any surprises, good or bad, that may arise. That way, your speakers and demo team are ready to respond right away to whatever might happen.

Problems come in many obvious shapes and forms, and like all problems, they will probably happen when you least expect them. Be well prepared for obvious issues like hardware or software failures, people problems, inadequate or failed/missing power, connectivity issues, lack of required outside interfaces, system crashes, display and/or audio system failures, and timing problems.

Chances are good that a well prepared and rehearsed demo won't have any problems, but as noted earlier in this book, Murphy's Law is alive and well. It always has been, and it always will be.

How to Handle an Issue or Problem

Rise to the Occasion and Shine!

So, what do you do when a problem raises its ugly head during your live demo? When this happens it truly becomes a test of your abilities, knowledge, composure, and backup plan. It also tests your team's flexibility and readiness to overcome adversity.

When problems occur, every person in the audience will give you their full attention. They will watch very closely to see how you react and what you will do. Because you've prepared for the unexpected and put contingency plans in place, this presents a unique opportunity for you and your team to shine. Yes, to really shine!

At the end of the "Prepare for Common and Uncommon Events" in Chapter 4, there is a story about a young program manager who became violently sick during a presentation. Take a look back at this story and note how the program manager composed himself and ultimately gained the respect and confidence of the audience.

When people problems are experienced during a live demo, remind yourself that we are all human and subject to vulnerabilities of many kinds. If you are alone, you must work through the issue yourself as best you can, however, during a team presentation, contingency planning demands that others come to your aid. When planned, this can be done smoothly, and your customer will see that your team is a real team that knows how to function as one.

But what do you do when you have an equipment or system failure? The first step is: Don't panic! Stop for a moment and collect your thoughts. Address your audience and use a phrase such as:

- "Let me go back a step or two and see if I can correct this issue."
- "You probably noticed that we've experienced an issue here. Let me see if I (or we) can quickly resolve it."
- "This issue was caused by ... so let me step back and correct it."
- "I'm not sure exactly what happened here. Teammate A or Teammate B (call out the person you need help from by name), can you help me out with this?"

If a really tough problem occurs and you and your teammates cannot correct it quickly, ask your customer if you can take a short break to assess what happened. There is nothing wrong with requesting a break, and your customer will respect you for asking. After the fix is found and made, explain to your audience exactly what happened. Doing this is vital and it will help to restore any lost confidence. Being able to identify, correct, and own a problem under extreme pressure during a live demo is a very desirable trait.

When a failure occurs and there appears to be no way to get back on track, fall back on other aspects of your contingency plan. Perhaps there are other features of your demo that can be completed or you can explain what issues you have found and discuss corrective measures you will take to correct them. Don't just give up!

As you would during execution of a real project, tell your customer what you will do to address and correct the problem so this won't happen again. Finally, after all other options have been exhausted, request a new time and date to complete your demo. Chances are your customer may respect your request, but if they do not, at least you asked the question.

Before Going Live — Holistic Review, Integration, and Rehearsal

Holistically Review Your Demo, Ensure That It's Logically Integrated, and Unmercifully Review It Again and Again

Now that you've planned all aspects of your demo, review it holistically for logical flow. Make sure your words, visuals, and actions are well coordinated.

Next, take a look at your demo in the context of your entire presentation. Ensure there are no contradictions or disconnects. Reflecting on your overall win strategy and value proposition, double check that your demo has leveraged your discriminators and your insights into customer needs, issues, hot buttons, and risks.

Rehearse your demo with an experienced, diverse, cross-functional, in-house audience that simulates your real audience and solicit their feedback. Include technical and nontechnical people, executives, and senior leaders, new-hires, and junior people, an equal mix of women and men, and by all means, a professional orals/speech coach.

Take their inputs very seriously, and constructively weave them into your presentation. You and your team may think you "know better," but be assured, you do not. The feedback that your practice audience provides you is extremely valuable. Addressing their concerns and constructive feedback will make your demo much better.

Celebrate Success!

One of the most important things proposal, presentation, and demo teams forget to do is to celebrate! You've worked hard to plan and create a winning demo. Now that you've completed this milestone, congratulate yourselves and thank all who helped out!

Chapter 7

Sample Charts

On the following pages you will find examples of how to structure your graphics so that they are easy to read and send positive messages that can stand alone without being verbally augmented by a speaker. The comments on each chart stress important aspects to make you aware of salient points and techniques that may not be obvious to a casual reader who quickly flips through them. All charts shown here are fictitious and unrelated to each other—that is, they contain standalone messaging not intended to show a logical build-up progression.

Using a graphic artist to format your charts is very important. Professionally prepared charts send a strong message to your audience, and conversely, poorly prepared charts send a strong message too! Do everything you can to make a positive impression on your audience including charts that look professional, are easy to read, and clearly support the winning messages that you are delivering.

There is always a temptation to start building charts too early in the process. Resist this temptation and ensure you know the message that each chart will support before you actually draft the chart. Professionally prepared charts are not cheap, and they require a great deal of time to generate. Eliminate waste and rework; think through your messages first, rely on your presentation outline for guidance, and be sure to include your win themes and discriminators throughout your presentation.

Master's Tip: There's No Substitute for Years of Successful Experience—Capitalize on these Winning Tips

Here are a few tips that will help to make your presentation a winner:

- Create a style guide, essentially a template, that the entire presentation will follow. Consistency across the entire presentation is important. The style guide specifies font sizes, colors, margins, chart numbering, and banners. In essence, it details every graphic aspect that all charts will have in common.
- Select a font that is easy to read from every position in the presentation room. Refer to the "Effective Graphics and Visuals" section in Chapter 3 for pointers on how to deal with color blindness or color deficiency.
- Ensure that your "takeaway" messages included at the bottom of each chart support your value proposition, win themes, and discriminators. Ask yourself, "What's the single message I would like the audience to remember from this chart?"
- Don't use overly automated chart build-up features. Overuse can quickly become distracting.

- Don't use red font or red take-away boxes. Red subconsciously says, "Stop." Use pleasing colors like green or blue instead. These colors subconsciously say, "Go."
- Don't cram too much on a slide. Less is better.
- Use photos and video when appropriate for maximum impact. Keep your presentation charts interesting. Make your audience want to see the next one!
- For our budget-conscious project leads, when new complex drawings or illustrations are needed, discourage your engineers and technical people from generating these drawings on a computer themselves. Encourage the originator to sketch it out on a piece of paper and hand it over to a professional CAD/graphic artist for finalization. Let's face it, it's a lot more cost effective and faster to have a graphic artist capture and generate an image electronically from a hand sketch than it is for a highly paid engineer to do so. The end result will be a better product too. Keep your engineers and technicians focused on creativity and resolving technical issues, not on drawing charts!

Overall Approach, Win Theme, and Discriminators Chart

The chart displayed in Figure 7.1 summarizes the overall approach to a project. Generally a chart like this is used to kick off a presentation. When it is well done and resonates with the customer, this may become the single chart that is associated with you and your approach.

The chart features your overall win theme and your discriminators. The words in the center represent the win theme, and the words around the perimeter are the enablers that you are offering.

The takeaway is easy to read and it captures the overall approach. Words and phrases are action oriented.

Figure 7.1 Sample Chart —Overall Approach, Win Theme, and Discriminators

Organizational Chart

Organizational charts can be overly complicated and often times confusing. It's always best to keep it simple and easy to understand (see Figure 7.2), regardless of the size or complexity of the project.

When you have teammates, subcontractors, suppliers, and vendors, highlight the key ones on your chart. This shows that you are indeed a team and that you understand successful project execution depends on good management with clear lines of reporting and responsibility.

Another good practice is to show the contractor reporting relationship with your customer. If you are certain of how this will work (and you should be based on preproposal discussions with your customer), you may choose to graphically show the relationship on the organizational chart. Doing this establishes lines of communication, reporting, and responsibility across the entire project.

Figure 7.2 Sample Chart—Organizational Chart

Impact and Special Messages Chart

Short, impactful video clips can make a point that won't be forgotten (see Figure 7.3). Be sure the video launches properly and the audio is clear. When using video clips, ensure that the content is appropriate for your audience and that the point is obvious to everyone. Before using a video, always test its use on your practice audience and get their feedback. If anyone in your practice audience doesn't get the point or is offended by the content in any way, don't use it.

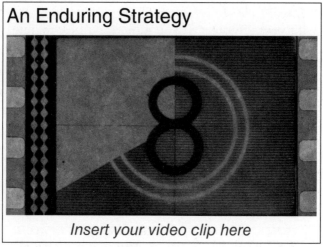

Figure 7.3   Sample Chart—Impact and Special Messages

Build-Up

Build-up charts can be very effective when your message and your timing are intelligently and logically thought out. In this initial section of the build-up chart (see Figure 7.4a), the message couldn't be clearer. The speaker is obviously talking about a loss and not punishing the failure – a sobering chart indeed.

The second part of this build-up chart, which appears with advancement to the next chart, (see Figure 7.4b addition to 7.4a), adds some words of wisdom. The impact of this is indeed profound and it's very likely that it will have a positive, uplifting impact on every person in your audience. Think through your build-up charts carefully and use them wisely!

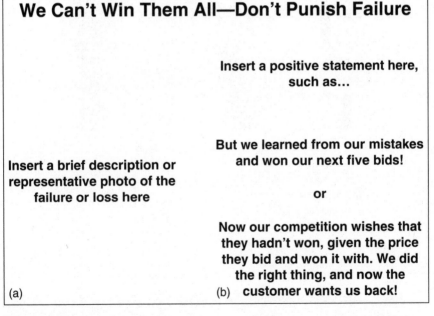

Figure 7.4 Build-Up Sample Charts

Text-Intensive Charts

Text-intensive charts should be avoided but are sometimes necessary (see Figure 7.5). Select your words carefully and ensure the chart doesn't become too cluttered or textually dense. Pick key words and address each one of them in your own words. When categorical sections are needed as in this sample chart, use color, text size, and underlining to separate the categories.

Finally, remember that every word on the chart must be easy to read from any position in your presentation room. If you can't see a word from the back of the room, make it bigger. If making it bigger clutters the chart or doesn't fit, generate another chart. All charts must be easy to read.

Our Best Practices & Approach

Program Management
- Comprehensive, Audited PM Processes
- PM Training
- Systems Integration / Engineering / Modeling
- Communication & Teamwork
- Customer Electronic Desktop
  - Full Visibility into Program
  - Metrics for Technical, Cost, & Schedule
  - Integrated Master Schedule
  - Risk Management Tool
- Business Case Analysis
- Corporate Reachback
- Environment, Health, & Safety

Human Resources
- Employee Retention
- Recruiting
- Resource Management
- Training

Technical
- Modern, Scalable Design
- Technology Insertion Plan
- Honest Broker
  - Prequalified Vendors
  - Compete All Buys
  - Leveraged Buying Practices
- IT Security
- Help Desk / Desktop Support

Outreach
- Educational
- Community

Proven to Save Money & Reduce Risk

Figure 7.5 Text-Intensive Sample Chart

Mixing Key Words and Graphics

Mixing key words such as features, discriminators, and benefits with well-chosen photographs, drawings, or illustrations is very effective (see Figure 7.6). Using this technique lets you talk to each key point, and the image tells a story as well.

In this example, teamwork is clearly the main theme and the chart expands on this by identifying additional components of teamwork that are important to the corporate culture. The words support the graphic, and the graphic supports the words. Meaningless images will detract from your presentation and can actually set up conflicting messages. Select your words and your graphics carefully and make sure they complement each other in a logical and meaningful way.

Figure 7.6 Mixing Key Words and Graphics

Sample Chart—Features and Benefits

Highlighting the features of your approach is good practice, but it's not enough! Sometimes we become so close to our approach we assume that the benefits to our customer are obvious. Be assured that this is *not* the case. Never ever assume that your audience understands the benefits of any feature or element of your approach.

Almost all of us have at one time or another been in a meeting or discussion where one person says, "Gee, I didn't think about that!" As you itemize your benefits to your customer, remember that they "may not have thought about that."

Always show your audience what you believe the benefits of your approach or solutions are to them (see Figure 7.7). Make sure that they tie back to key requirements, customer hot buttons, and your discriminators. Keep in mind that a single feature can lead to multiple benefits. As shown in this sample chart, there are more benefits listed than there are features. This is okay, and is in fact, a very good thing indeed.

Figure 7.7 Features and Benefits Sample Chart

Risks Chart

In complex programs, address key risks directly (see Figure 7.8). Anyone who has made a financial investment or major purchase of any kind understands the importance of risk identification and how risks can be mitigated or eliminated. Identify each risk and then assess the impact it can have on the project if it isn't mitigated. Next tell what you are doing to address each risk and what the resultant risk will be after your mitigation techniques are applied.

You will never convince everyone that you can completely eliminate a major risk. There are always skeptics in the audience, so never say that there is no risk. Reduce risks by applying proven mitigation techniques and approaches.

Be careful not to identify too many risks. Select those that are blatantly obvious, that your customer believes exist, and that may be unique to your *competitor's* approach.

Risks & Risk Mitigation

Risk	Risk Assessment	Risk Mitigation Approach	Resultant Risk
Transition	Medium	Proven Dedicated Transition Team; Phase-Out Plan	Low
Human Resources	High	Retain Qualified Candidates; Draw Upon Corporate Resources	Low
Program Integration	Medium	Common Understanding of Requirements; Communication; Incentives; Transparency	Low
Project Management	Medium	Project Management Plans; Electronic Desktop; Well Defined Processes; Training; New App	Low
Logistics / Supply Chain	High	Reduction of Inventory Levels; Just in Time; Automated Processes; Asset Visibility	Medium

Our Risk Management Plan Addresses & Mitigates All Risks

Figure 7.8 Risks Chart

Financial and Statistical Charts

Financial and statistical charts (see Figures 7.9 and 7.10) of any kind can easily overwhelm an audience if they are not done properly. Keep them as simple as possible and keep them legible. If tables, histograms, or line graphs are used, be sure they can be read from every position in the presentation room.

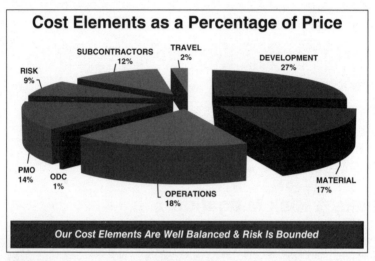

Figure 7.9   A Sample Financial Chart

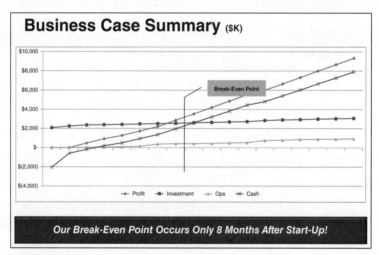

Figure 7.10   A Sample Statistical Chart

Tables

Tables can quickly become boring. Use a variety of graphic techniques to help keep them interesting and help your audience navigate them more easily. In the sample chart shown in Figure 7.11, you could insert company logos into the large blue boxes to make it more interesting while adding company branding at the same time. Get creative and keep your audience's attention!

Figure 7.11   A Sample Table

Technical Illustrations and Drawings

Engineers, technicians, designers, and technical people of all kinds take great pride in their drawings and illustrations. One of the most difficult things to do in a presentation is to take their raw input and insert it into the presentation so that it communicates to the audience properly. The key is to simplify as much as possible without diminishing the technical content (see Figure 7.12).

In some cases using multiple charts may be the answer. Using chart animation features to blow up each section of a detailed illustration is also very effective. Handing out a hard copy of a complex drawing to each member of the audience is another good way to go when projection of large illustrations becomes awkward.

No matter what technique you use, test it out on your practice audience and see how they react. Ask if the right messages have been conveyed and ask if there are suggestions for improvement.

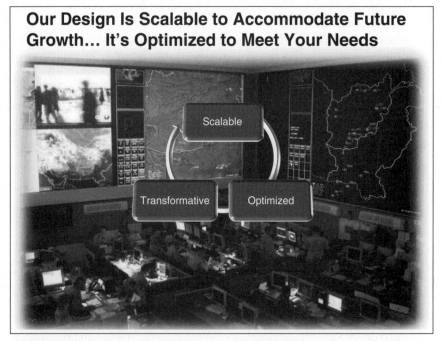

Figure 7.12   Sample Technical Illustrations and Drawings

Appendix

Federal Acquisition Regulation (FAR) 15.102 Oral Presentations

(a) Oral presentations by offerors as requested by the government may substitute for or augment written information. Use of oral presentations as a substitute for portions of a proposal can be effective in streamlining the source selection process. Oral presentations may occur at any time in the acquisition process, and they are subject to the same restrictions as written information, regarding timing (see FAR 15.208) and content (see FAR 15.306). Oral presentations provide an opportunity for dialogue among the parties. Pre-recorded videotaped presentations that lack real-time interactive dialogue are not considered oral presentations for the purposes of this section, although they may be included in offeror submissions, when appropriate.

(b) The solicitation may require each offeror to submit part of its proposal through oral presentations. However, representations and certifications shall be submitted as required in the FAR provisions at 52.204-8(d) or 52.212-3(b), and a signed offer sheet (including any exceptions to the government's terms and conditions) shall be submitted in writing.

(c) Information pertaining to areas such as an offeror's capability, past performance, work plans or approaches, staffing resources, transition plans, or sample tasks (or other types of tests) may be suitable for oral presentations. In deciding what information to obtain through an oral presentation, consider the following:

1. The government's ability to adequately evaluate the information.
2. The need to incorporate any information into the resultant contract.
3. The impact on the efficiency of the acquisition.
4. The impact (including cost) on small businesses. In considering the costs of oral presentations, contracting officers should also consider alternatives to on-site oral presentations (e.g., teleconferencing, video teleconferencing).

(d) When oral presentations are required, the solicitation shall provide offerors with sufficient information to prepare them. Accordingly, the solicitation may describe—

1. The types of information to be presented orally and the associated evaluation factors that will be used;
2. The qualifications for personnel that will be required to provide the oral presentation(s);
3. The requirements for, and any limitations and/or prohibitions on, the use of written material or other media to supplement the oral presentations;
4. The location, date, and time for the oral presentations;
5. The restrictions governing the time permitted for each oral presentation; and
6. The scope and content of exchanges that may occur between the government's participants and the offeror's representatives as part of the oral presentations, including whether or not discussions (see FAR 15.306(d)) will be permitted during oral presentations.

(e) The contracting officer shall maintain a record of oral presentations to document what the government relied upon in making the source selection decision. The method and level of detail of the record (e.g., videotaping, audio tape recording, written record, government notes, copies of offeror briefing slides or presentation notes) shall be at the discretion of the source selection authority. A copy of the record placed in the file may be provided to the offeror.

(f) When an oral presentation includes information that the parties intend to include in the contract as material terms or conditions, the information shall be put in writing. Incorporation by reference of oral statements is not permitted.

(g) If, during an oral presentation, the government conducts discussions (see FAR 15.306(d)), the government must comply with FAR 15.306 and FAR 15.307.

Acknowledgments

Special appreciation to Judy Smyer, Allen Badeau, Sue Shaffer, Peter Stewart, and Daniel Stewart for their tireless help in reviewing and editing the content of this book. Your feedback and suggestions have helped make this book a stronger coaching guide for teams at any stage of experience along the orals path. Our sincere thanks for your time and your wisdom!

We would also like to thank Pat and Kevin Sullivan of Sullivan & Associates for their photographic assistance and support. Of course, we also extend our thanks to the employees of this fine organization who were drafted into posing for the photos!

About the Authors

John Parker Stewart

John has worked with proposals and proposal teams for over 35 years. He began his career as a Lockheed executive in the 1970s. In 1980 he started his own consulting firm where he has coached and trained Fortune 500 companies in capturing multimillion and billion dollar government contracts and then delivering effective performance by leveraging successful management and leadership practices. He specializes in providing orals coaching to proposal teams of all sizes and levels of experience.

John was selected as the Association for Talent Development's national Trainer of the Year for two consecutive years. He has coached and trained thousands of CEOs, presidents, executives, professionals, astronauts, and military leaders in communication, presentation, and team leadership skills. His clients work with DOD, DOE, NASA, all military branches, other government agencies, and commercial firms.

His publications include "Orals Coaching: The Secret Weapon for Winning Contracts" in the Association for Proposal Management Professionals' journal *Proposal Management*. He is a three-time speaker on Orals Coaching and Contract Capture at APMP's National Conference. He has published several award winning leadership books. Among his primary clients are Lockheed Martin, Raytheon, Boeing, Northrop Grumman, BAE Systems, CACI, the US Air Force, Kennedy Space Center, and Johnson Space Center.

John lives with his wife, Debra, near Portland, Oregon.

Donald Fulop

Born in Wisconsin and blessed to be raised in a home on the shore of Okauchee Lake, Don went on to enjoy a 40-year career equally divided between engineering, program management, and business development. Starting at Rockwell-Collins in avionics engineering, followed by a decade of productive years in program management at Harris Corporation, Don then joined Lockheed Martin. After 25 years of service at Lockheed in programs and business development, he retired as a VP in their National Intelligence business area.

He then rode his Harley around our great country for the better part of two years before joining CACI as executive vice president of business development following gentle but persistent coaxing from their CEO, Ken Asbury. He remained with CACI for three years where he built up their business development expertise; successfully championed continued growth in existing markets; and penetrated new, unserved markets. He was also key in closing several M&A actions valued in excess of $1 billion.

Over Don's career in business development, he led teams that secured over $16 billion in new business and did so with a win/capture rate that was consistently 20–25% above industry average. He has worked with foreign and domestic commercial customers, foreign governments, the U.S. National Intelligence Community, the Department of Defense (DOD),

Defense Advanced Research Projects Agency (DARPA), Department of State (DOS), Drug Enforcement Agency (DEA), Department of Justice (DOJ), and many federal civilian agencies such as National Aeronautics and Space Administration (NASA), the Veterans Administration (VA), and the National Science Foundation (NSF).

He has worked virtually every aspect of ground and space-based advanced communications and IT systems including design, development, production, and postdeployment product support. Don credits his success to strategic thinking, carefully listening to the thoughts and opinions of others, and application of processes proven and honed over decades, many aspects of which are shared in this book.

Don earned a BS degree at the University of Wisconsin and MS and MBA degrees from the Florida Institute of Technology. He is a DoD Program Management graduate of the Defense Systems Management College at Fort Belvoir, Virginia, and he is a US patent holder.

Don lives with his beautiful wife Maryann in Colorado Springs, where he continues to ride his Harley and occasionally wets a line in a few of the many rivers and lakes that grace the State of Colorado.

Index